Copyright © 2004 by Scott Schultz

All rights reserved. No part of this publication may be reproduced or transmitted in any form or by any means, electronic or mechanical, including photocopy, recording, or any information storage and retrieval system, without permission in writing from the publisher.

ISBN 1-930596-30-8

Published by THE GUEST COTTAGE, INC.
PO Box 848
Woodruff, WI 54568
1-800-333-8122

www.theguestcottage.com

Printed in Canada

Rural Routes & Ruts
Roaming the Roads of Rural Life

by Scott Schultz

The Guest Cottage Inc.
dba Amherst Press

Dedication

Dedicated to the three people who pointed me down the road that led me to writing this book:

My mother, Virgina, who first taught me the joys of reading, paying attention to my surroundings and using my imagination.

Marvelene Butterbrodt, a beloved teacher who pushed me to write and then encouraged me to make it my profession.

Sybil Basombrio, a teacher who showed me how to enjoy the creative side of the human spirit and include it in my writing.

Contents

Foreword . . . . **page viii**
    Finding Ways to be 'Used Up'

Rural Routes . . . . **page 1**
    A Rural Route

Rural Route 1 - A Family Journey . . . . **page 5**
    A Move Henry Would Make
    Return Routes
    Talking Turkey with Dad on a Bright Spring Morning
    Rural Survival Rules (Please)
    Fighting the Forces of Gravity
    A License to Rubberneck
    Slips of the Knife
    The War of Birds
    Finding the Way to the Target
    Company on a Country Walk
    The Lessons of Death's Gifts
    Close Clips at Harry's and Mary's
    Building Big Bridges

Rural Route 2 - People Along the Route . . . . **page 45**
    Knowing Great People
    Warmth with Rural Secrets
    The Rural Chase
    Hanging with Johnny Possum and Turtle Head
    Dale's Heroic Lesson
    A Sad Time for Funeral Foods
    The Country Doctor
    Harry Puts Up the 'Closed' Sign
    Getting a Gizzard Check
    Alfred was a Fair Man
    Playing Through Pain
    Falling and Rising with a November Full Moon
    A Trophy Message
    Rural Routes of the Heart

Rural Route 3 - Rural Elements . . . . page 77
   Facing January from a Barn Door
   Gems from the Country Sky
   Simple Things in Life Appreciated
   Beauty in Sight Only
   Games Played with the Moon's Brightness
   Spring Will Win the Fight
   Spring's Arrival on the Wing
   The Spring Songs of Frogs
   A Good Place for Purification
   Where the Stars Shine Brightly
   Feeling Freedom in a New Pasture
   A Rocky Conversation
   June Mornings Don't Last Forever
   Fully Exposed to Life
   The Wonder of Nothing
   Nights of Rural Route Drama
   Hummingbirds in a World of Eagles
   Chirp of the Crickets
   Reflections of the Dog Days
   Tenacititis Bolditriticus Stickinfinitum
   New, Old Worries in the Woods
   Splendor in the Northern Sky
   The Woods' Sound of Silence
   The Call of the Geese
   Leaves in the Woods
   The Land's Love isn't Jealous

Rural Route 4 - Rural Necessities . . . . page 121
   The Good of Being Born in a Barn
   Important Farm Tools
   Cutting Through the Myths of Work
   A Farm's Fossils
   Places to Hide
   A Little Church's Story in Me
   The Land vs. the Sprawl Beast
   Painting the Face of Rural Life
   Only a Tractor

Rural Ruts . . . . page 143
   Staying in a Rut

Acknowledgments . . . . page 146

Foreword

Finding Ways to be 'Used Up'

Someone asked a while back, tongue-in-cheek – I think – whether I'd started to have my "mid-life crisis."

I had, after all, officially hit my mid-40s, as age goes. And, that's the time when men commonly are viewed as having lost most of their senses with the signaling of the official departure of their youth.

In recent months, I've been giving plenty of thought to why men would tend to do seemingly strange things at this age, and some recent events have led me to some conclusions.

Among the foremost of those conclusions is to throw out the idea that the "crisis" for men my age has primarily to do with their loss of youth. Instead, I think it has to do with the realization that there isn't a lot of time left to accomplish some of the meaningful and well-intended things that we'd aimed to accomplish.

A common refrain heard by guys my age, I think, is that "you've changed." I'm not certain how exactly I may have changed, other than in terms of the obvious physical changes.

I loved athletics and hunting when I was 18; I love them and compete now. I loved youthful exuberance when I was 18; I love it now.

When I was 18, I loved hearing and taking on a challenge such as "you can't do that." I still jump at the chance to prove doubters wrong. In fact, that sort of a challenge was a major reason for me having joined the Marine Corps (*maybe*, if you work hard enough, you can be one of *us*). These days, it's a reason why I still, at 5-10 and 210 pounds (not exactly a runner's physique), tie on running shoes to run a couple of 26.2 mile full marathons each year.

If there have been changes, perhaps they have been the results of the time I've spent observing and listening to people and things. Hours spent working with people from all backgrounds and attitudes can help you to be a real "people person," and the hours I've spent on my stump in my Veefkind woods to contemplate life helps one to develop some focus. I think, overall, that could be seen as little more than maturing through life's experiences.

What really strikes me more, though, is the gnawing urge to get those important jobs done.

As part of that process called "life experience," you get to see life as being unfairly short. That process, for me, started with the death of my pal and cousin, Kenny, who left us when I was only 6 years old – he was but a year older. At 18, I watched as Dick, a high school pal who drowned at a pre-graduation party, was lowered into his grave. While in the Marine Corps, I was part of honor guards for the funerals of too many Marines who departed in their prime. And, in the past few years, I've seen the deaths of my mother, my father, a sister, my mother-in-law, a sister-in-law, a brother-in-law, two uncles and a cousin.

All of their losses carried with them grief at varied levels. But, perhaps one of the most poignant moments came upon the unexpected death of my sister. Upon receiving notification of her death while I was at work, I sat for a few minutes with our newspaper's editor, who is about my age. There, we decided we both had hit the age when such calls were going to come all too often.

I'm not asking for sympathy. I have gone through grief in each case and think I've come to understand that process. Faith in a life hereafter has been important. Also, realize that plenty of folks in my circles have lived much longer lives.

I'm asking for more understanding for guys when they reach the age I'm entering. More than anything, experiences such as the deaths of people, the likes of which I've seen, have shown me – and others like me – that we'd better get going and live *now*.

George Bernard Shaw wrote, *"This is the true joy in life – that being used for a purpose recognized by yourself as a mighty one. That being a force of nature, instead of a feverish, selfish little clod of ailments and grievances complaining that the world will not devote itself to making you happy. I am of the opinion that my life belongs to the whole community and as long as I live it is my privilege to do for it whatever I can. I want to be thoroughly used up when I die. For the harder I work the more I live. I rejoice in life for its own sake. Life is no brief candle to me. It's a sort of splendid torch which I've got to hold up for a moment and I want to make it burn as brightly as possible before handing it on to future generations."*

With that in mind, please excuse me and other fellas my age if we appear to be scrambling to get a few extra things done. It may include going on a trip; it may involve spending a little extra time with loved ones. Some may want to parachute for the first time; perhaps some will make a career change, or work on projects to share knowledge with others. Maybe it will mean spending more time sitting on a stump, listening to the birds and drinking in the smell of a woodlot.

It certainly will include writing about things I've learned along the way, sharing with people who haven't been able to experience the wonder of my rural world. That's the task I'm hoping to accomplish by putting together this collection of rural experiences.

My focus is on a place called Veefkind, a once-thriving little farm community in central Wisconsin. Little is left there besides a couple of farms, a cemetery that holds many of my ancestors, and several generations of memories.

"Rural route" was what the U.S. Postal Service used for country homes' addresses. For people like me, however, rural route means much more. It also refers to the direction – the route – I've taken in life because of experiences I've had in rural areas.

I've been told how many rural people seem to be in a "rural rut." I don't think that's always such a bad place to be, as long as we know when to leave our ruts to assure we accomplish all that's possible.

And, we should never apologize for wanting to accomplish tasks that are close to our hearts.

It's OK if you do fault me for following my *Rural Routes and Ruts* in hopes of doing all I can to live a full life. Life experience has warned me how some people find such fault. But, when someone receives the notification that my time has come, they'll at least know that I'd tried my best to be "used up" at the end.

Rural Routes and Ruts will always be part of me, however they're viewed.

Roaming the Roads of Rural Life

Rural Routes

A Rural Route

They called it a "rural route," the place named Veefkind, near the middle of Wisconsin.

It's no longer called that. The formalities of addresses have taken the "route" out of our rural lives. In doing so, I'm convinced that they've also changed the course – the route – of the directions rural people take.

The change has put the rural world into a rut much like the rut so often traveled by those in urban and suburban worlds.

Disappearing are the days when rural people wake to experience new wonders in their world. Increasing numbers of rural people find themselves rising to make a commute to work in their metropolitan world, never really feeling all that there is to feel on what had once been someone's rural route.

Get up. Go to work. Toil through the morning. Have lunch. Toil through the afternoon. Drive home.

For many, their days are directed in a single path, the same way that the mudded ruts on early rural roads kept Model T Fords moving in a single direction. And, like driving in those ruts, those people find that theirs is a no-win proposition: either their lives' vehicles start dragging bottom or – if they can somehow steer out of their ruts – they'll become stuck in new dirt.

Sure, they'll live the high life of being able to call themselves "rural." But they won't be any more rural than a country music star who grew up on the streets of metropolitan Dallas. That will be fine for them, but those who have never entered a rural rut or those who have found their personal rural route will take pity.

Those people who understand rural routes have a feeling for all that's wonderful about their world. They know the satisfaction of hands cracked and hardened from long days of labor. They've taken time to hold a handful of black dirt to their face to inhale its richness. They've known the feeling of standing barefoot in a fresh, warm cow pie on a cool June morning.

Rural routes are best found by people who have been chilled by shoes and pants wetted by dew from having herded cows from a pasture early in the morning. No matter where they travel, they will have the urge to stop to inhale the smell of a newly-cut hayfield. They will know the difference between the sound of corn leaves in late July and the sound of those same leaves in October.

Neighbors know neighbors on a rural route. They work with each other. They talk with each other. They pray with each other. They play with each other. Together, they share the joys of life and the sorrows of death.

Small churches dot corners in the world of those who know rural routes. Those churches, and sometimes small feed mills, often were the last-standing community structures in places like my rural Veefkind home. Family cemeteries generally are the only remaining evidence that small rural communities such as Veefkind ever existed.

Rural routes are about people, land, and animals.

People who understand rural routes know that animals, domestic and wild, can live well in the countryside. They know the most humane treatment of an animal might mean having to kill it. They've known and seen how their food is produced. They know that a well-treated animal generally returns the favor. They've seen and not panicked about the rather undesirable morsels being dragged around by a farm dog.

People who have lived on and traveled rural routes are willing to sample dishes developed to waste nothing. They may not eat it, but they understand and respect those who eat the likes of head cheese, sheep testicles, blood sausage, pickled tongue, boiled gizzards or fried beef heart.

Along their rural routes, people who haven't known rural ruts know of days when fenceline to fenceline farming and housing developments allowed habitats for ring-necked pheasants, bluebirds, meadowlarks and red-winged blackbirds. Brush piles in woodlots created an environment in which teenaged boys and their trusty beagles could flush and harvest rabbits.

The people of rural routes would prefer a world in which a few dairy cows, an acre or two of vegetables, some pasture, some chickens, some hogs and maybe a couple of farm geese – or even a turkey – would suffice. Though economics may have pushed them to a world of expanded, monocultural agriculture, their hearts lie in the days of small farms.

Taking rural routes, even longing for rural routes, isn't for everybody, I'd guess. Some people are satisfied only to know that they've been able to build their prized rural dream home on a pristine wooded hillside. They may not care about or consider the rural routes that touched their property.

That, to me, isn't what rural living is all about.

Rural routes have come to have too many meanings for me to allow me to stop using all of my senses to absorb the countryside. Just as Rural Route 2 once identified me and my Veefkind neighbors in the form of a mailing address, trying to find a different way – a new route – to feel rural life, has become my identity.

In some ways, that puts me in a rural rut as much as those country dwellers who simply aim to make their way through a daily routine. But as I explore my rural identity, at least I'll have been satisfied in having mapped my own rural routes.

Roaming the Roads of Rural Life

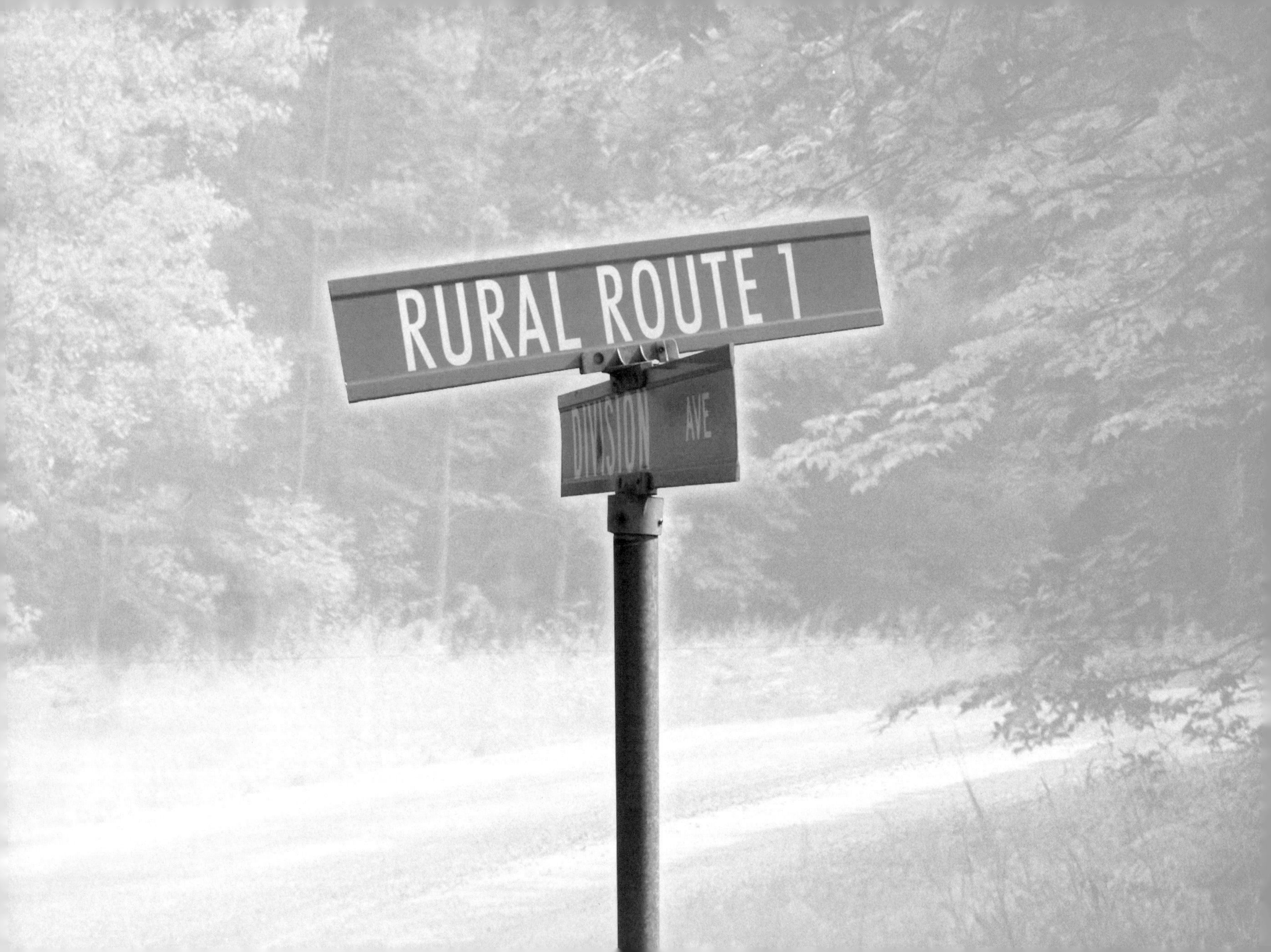
RURAL ROUTE 1
DIVISION AVE

A Family Journey

A Move Henry Would Approve

It's unlikely that Henry Veefkind would begrudge somebody moving away from his old farm.

That didn't make it any easier the day Henry's great grandson moved off the land where they had both spent the better parts of their lives trying to scrape out a living.

Howard moved into an apartment in town, just a few miles from the old home farm. It's about 9 miles, to be precise. But, for him, those few miles probably seemed like a few thousand miles.

It was the sort of move that isn't taken lightly by a family in which the fellow being moved grew up on that farm and then raised his own family there. It's a farm where Howard's great-grandfather, Henry, settled after arriving from Holland during the mid-1800s; a place where his grandparents, his parents, he and his wife, one of his sons, and one of his granddaughters had farmed.

There was very little time when Howard had been away from the place: a short time while he worked on another farm about 100 miles away in southern Wisconsin, a short time when he worked with a Civilian Conservation Corps crew, and a couple of years when he worked with his county's highway crew. Even during his time away from the farm, it continued to be part of his world, with either his parents or his brother working the land.

The farm never got to be anything special. It wasn't the type of place you'd consider for any of the major farm expositions, for sure. Still, it was home to Howard for most of his life, and he'd become comfortable being there.

He'd become versed in telling about how Henry Veefkind obtained the land from Cornell University, which had owned it through the government's land-grant university program. He told how the small community called Veefkind was established around the farm, complete with its railroad station, lumber mills, general store and post office. He talked about the boarding house that would become the farmhouse where he raised his own family and in which some of his own great-grandchildren would live.

He always seemed comfortable with the idea that a railroad spur-line had cut across the farm's front yard, a reminder of the days when the small community thrived on its own.

One summer day in his later years, one of Howard's sons suggested that his family purchase a quiet lake cabin for Howard to spend some of his retirement years.

"Shhhhhhh. Listen," Howard said. "What do you hear?"

"Nothing, I guess," the son said after pausing a few moments to listen to the quiet of the rural world.

"Why would I want to go someplace and hear people with boats or to have neighbors in the next lake lot?" Howard said. "I have all the quiet I need right here."

But, as much as it was part of him, age made it less physically comfortable for Howard to live there during his later years. It was hard for his children to watch him have to slow down, remembering distant days of seeing their father doing a little dance on the large wood furnace register after "firing up" on cold mornings.

If he cursed in those later years, it was about not being able to pick up his feet the way he thought he should be able to when climbing the steps and going into his house. Or, he might have been heard grumbling when he was trying to get up from his recliner to go to the kitchen table for visits with friends and family.

The move was a long time in the making. He and his wife, Virginia, were considering such a move a few years earlier when Virginia's failing health was making it difficult for them to live at their rural route.

The reality of the risks of the old couple living there was deeply understood by all. But they were risks that didn't seem to weigh heavily on Howard's or Virginia's minds.

"Dad, what if you and Ma were going someplace in the middle of the winter and you had a heart attack?" one of their daughters scolded. "Ma would fall down in the snow while she tried to help you, and there you'd both lie all night! What would happen then!?"

Howard took a few seconds to consider such a scenario.

"Huh. I guess they'd find us dead in the morning, and then have a funeral for us a couple of days later," he said, matter-of-factly.

After Virginia's death, Howard remained adamant for a couple of years about wanting to continue living there. After all, despite his own health problems, Virginia was no longer there to take care of, and he was quite sure he could take care of himself. Besides, there was plenty of help when he'd need it, with most of his children living nearby.

But he eventually saw the need for a move. His apartment in town would have plenty of conveniences that would make his life easier. And, it's close enough to his family's farming operations that he'd be able to drive for visits to the farms – and maybe even to offer his opinions on what should be going on at those farms.

Howard's children all expressed their understanding about his emotions surrounding the move, but it was difficult, even for them. One day before the move, Howard told his youngest son that he'd been looking out of a window at the woods north of his house; that he'd been watching a flock of geese feeding in a nearby cornfield. He'd miss sights like that, he surmised.

When Virginia died, he told his children how his life had passed by so quickly.

Henry Veefkind and his daughter, Rika.

"Here I am, only 80 years old, and I feel like I'm in my 20s with a lot to get done yet," he said.

His son assured Howard that his children would get him out to see that view of the woods, to those geese, and to see how the corn was doing. Living conditions in the apartment would make life more comfortable, the son said – trying to reassure himself and his father.

It was, indeed, a move that Howard needed to make and which would, indeed, make Howard's life more comfortable.

The son understood how it was a move Howard had dreaded for so long and a move that so many others like Howard had dreaded.

Leaving the soil is never an easy thing.

As the son drove past the Veefkind cemetery a quarter-mile from the old home farm, he glanced toward Henry Veefkind's grave. The son wondered what Henry would say about all of the fretting regarding leaving the farm. Henry's grave was that of a man who left his homeland and traveled many miles with his family to find happiness – and just happened to settle on a few acres that became Howard's home place.

The son suspected that Henry would remind his descendants that people came from the dust and would return to the dust soon enough. In the meantime, it would be OK for folks like Howard to move his dust from one place to another.

Or, maybe Henry would say that if people respect the soil enough, the soils won't allow them to sink so far into it that they can't move their feet.

Maybe Henry would tell Howard and his children to scoop some soil into a jar and carry it with them as they started another journey, just to remember where they'd been.

Henry, the son thought, would give his approval to Howard's move – and maybe even wonder what took so long to make it.

Return Routes

I don't know why I ever left. Veefkind had everything I'd ever wanted – the land, the air, the creatures, the people.

When you're 18, though, the world is yours. You take your invincible being and head into the world to make a bigger and better life for yourself.

Before then, I'd seen my father cry only twice. Once was when he was told that his father had died. The second time was at his mother's funeral.

The third time was the day a U.S. Marine Corp recruiter waited for my family and friends to say goodbye to me before the recruiter drove me to a bus station to start my tour in Uncle Sam's service.

I wear my emotions on my sleeve, so crying has never been a big deal from my perspective. But for my father – a man who was raised to believe that men shouldn't cry – it was a big deal.

That afternoon had been quite a celebration; family, friends and neighbors had gathered for beer and food in the front yard where my great-great grandfather, Henry Borne Veefkind, had built a farm 100 years earlier. We joked. We smiled. We laughed.

Then, the recruiter came. My departure from my rural roots became real as he asked whether I was ready to go. Dad, whose previous physical contact with me had centered on disciplinary matters, suddenly became another person.

The Vietnam War was just ending. His closest contact with the military service had been through his uncle, Edward, whose remains are in France – a casualty of World War I.

In recent years, he had known 18-year-old boys who left home and who returned as changed men; maybe troubled; maybe sick. Or dead.

Dad's emotions and fears were justified by the measure of any caring parent, but certainly unexpected by me, considering the sensible approach to life that was common in Veefkind.

He hugged me.

He cried.

He told me that he loved me.

I'm not sure whether I'd really even meant to leave. Joining the Marine Corps had been the result of a dare of a high school friend. I'd signed out of a psychology class with a few other friends to see a Navy recruiter, which disrupted a test to have been given that day.

"I don't know why you guys went to see that recruiter," the friend said. "You don't have any intention of joining the service. You only screwed things up for the rest of us because so many of you went to see that recruiter."

My friend was right in many respects. I really hadn't intended to join any service. More than likely, I'd thought I'd simply sign on to play football at some college and eventually find my way into a writing career.

But to prove my friend wrong, I went to see another recruiter – the one from the Marine Corps. That was a mistake, because he was everything that a Marine Corps recruiter should be. He was spit-shined and polished from head to foot, and his presence showed me the difference in expectations that the Marine Corps held when compared with other military branches. In other words, he was "tight."

The topper was a poster with a Marine Corps drill instructor nose-to-nose with a recruit. The caption over the photo, which clearly had the drill instructor screaming in the recruit's face, was a take-off of a popular song of that era: "I beg your pardon; we don't promise you a rose garden."

Other than what I'd experienced in school settings, Veefkind and its simple rural life had been all that I'd known. A couple of visits to an uncle's house in southeastern Wisconsin, some college football games and trips to state track, wrestling and forensic competitions in Madison had been my contact with the "world." In fact, they'd been my only contact with people of color.

But I feared nothing, at least until Dad's hug, tears and words made the seriousness of my actions really hit home.

Every generation, in every part of the country, undoubtedly has a large percentage of youth who are ready to leave their home, prepared to return only for brief visits. I may have been included in that percentage, since I would have been leaving home for a college had it not been for my travels with the Marine Corps.

When people reach that age, they make one of three choices: stay home to pursue their dreams; leave and never look back; or leave with future options remaining open.

I knew from the start that I'd be among those who would leave home with future options remaining open.

It amazes me to this day that I ever left in the first place. The dairy farm is what I knew. Even at a young age, I could feel a pulse for the land. There certainly were jobs on the farm that I didn't like to do, but for the most part, Veefkind's soil had been stuck beneath my fingernails in more ways than one.

I remember challenging my oldest brother one night, two years before joining the Marine Corps, with the idea that I'd someday work at a desk job while he and others in the family continued to toil on their farms. He and his wife only laughed at my contention and agreed that I'd "be there with the rest of us."

I went from coast to coast. I went to the Far East.

When all was said and done, I saw no place that fit me better than Wisconsin's dirt.

I'm not sure whether I'd be able to describe what makes a place "home." In my case, I know it's a place in which I feel comfortable writing about its people and places. It's a place in which I'm familiar with the bumps of so many rural roads; a place in which I'm familiar with the sights, sounds and smells.

Others might find "home" in places far from the place where they'd been raised. If I'd tried, I wouldn't have been able to deny my home.

I know it as a place where people generally are honest in their feelings for me and for the land.

The honesty that Dad – truly a man of the soil – had for me through his tears so many years ago told me I should be back there, near the place my ancestors also called "home."

I'll continue to travel elsewhere. I'll continue to return.

Homes in rural places treat us that way.

I don't know why I left, but I know why I returned.

Talking Turkey with Dad on a Bright Spring Morning

Hunting turkeys isn't a popular endeavor within our family. It hasn't been too many years since turkeys had again — if they ever previously had — started to populate the land in and around my beloved Veefkind woods.

Most of my family has carried on the hunting tradition in other forms, seeking out small game and big game species across the countryside. I hold the tradition closely to my heart for its ability to get me into the natural world. The harvest, for me, is a bonus.

I'd watched with wonder as the turkey population grew around Veefkind during the past few years.

Like the whitetail population, the turkey population had grown to the point where some management of their numbers was needed.

Being part of a spring turkey hunt could be quite a pleasant experience, I surmised. I've made a habit of visiting my woods one or two days in April or May for no other reason than to lean against the south side of an oak tree, to drink in the spring sun's warmth, and to inhale the intoxicating cleanliness of the spring air.

Maybe I believed that by carrying a slate turkey call, a couple of decoys and a 12-gauge shotgun into the woods I would be better able to justify my time there.

Certainly, there would be the challenge of the hunt, but still it was that springtime visit to the woods that made my pulse race as much as the thought of bagging a turkey.

The timing for my hunt couldn't have been better, I knew. It coincided with the first anniversary of my father's death. If I situated myself correctly in my woods, I knew that I'd be able to catch an occasional glimpse of the Veefkind Cemetery down the road. That's the place that holds the remains of my ancestors from great-great grandfather Hendrick Veefkind to my parents. I could also see the farm that Hendrick had built and on which I was raised.

My first turkey hunt quickly became a great tool for some of the most profound contemplation and reflection that I ever was able to muster.

I turned my attention to the east, toward the sunrise that opened the bright, blue sky over the cemetery and the Veefkind farm. It didn't take me long to "see" Dad, even at that distance, stalking across the farm's yard, heading toward the barn for the morning milking.

His stride contained a mix of anger and disgust over my dislike for having to jump from bed to get some work done before heading off to school. His fingers, some of them already crooked from the challenges of hard work he'd done in his early years, straightened and then fisted as he worked to make the yellow chore gloves feel comfortable on his broad hands. The vision took me back many years; many more years than I'd care to even admit.

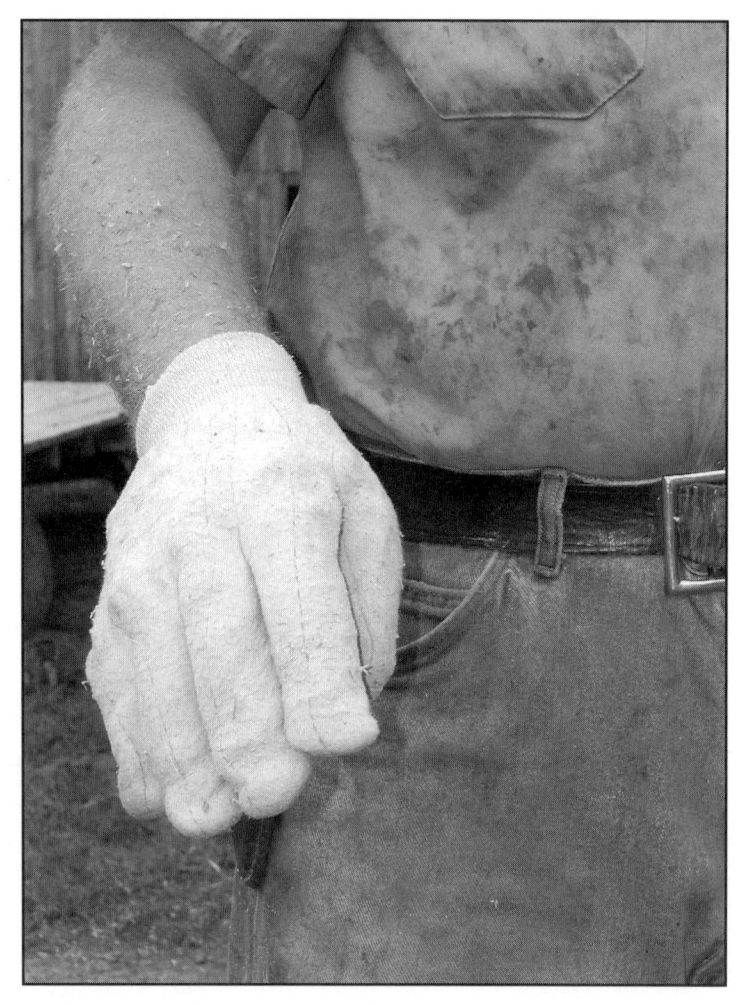

I knew all he wanted was for me to do what was right. I knew he needed the help even my body — so young at the time — could provide. I knew my belligerence had aged his heart beyond its years.

A smile came to my face, and an audible laugh burst from me as I realized how, in his later years, he was amused that I had no problem bounding from a bed when harassed by a Marine Corps drill instructor, or when the matter involved an early-morning visit to the woods.

My response to his laughter was to say it was "my job" to make my belligerence part of his morning routine – similar to my stealing the Saltine crackers that he would carefully butter and organize around his soup bowl. It seemed to be a challenge to see whether we could break each other's will with the morning routine, and a challenge to see whether I could get his crackers away before he could rap my knuckles with his butter knife.

I dozed against a tree as the vision of his stride was still fresh in my mind.

The second day of my turkey hunt would bring new visions of my father.

Dad had slipped away from his pain and away from this world exactly a year from that second hunting day, and my mind was occupied with that as I deployed my trusty decoys.

As the sun rose that morning over the Veefkind farm and the cemetery, my sense of the mixture of past, present and future was stronger than it had ever been in the woods. I used my ungloved hand to reach for the ground as I sat against my tree, grasping a handful of nearly decayed leaves and some of the soil under them.

As with my ancestors, the leaves' history has deeply enriched that soil. Together, they've given great strength to the oak upon which I leaned and to my bond with that soil.

Dad never had the chance to hunt turkeys. But, he hunted with me as I harvested a turkey on that second day. As I picked up my bounty and headed east toward my truck, I looked up and saw another vision of my father walking across the farm's yard. This time, though, he stopped and turned around to see what I'd done.

His early-morning troubled look softened, and a smirk creased from the corner of his mouth.

"Well, I'll be damned," he said. "See what happens when you get out of bed at a decent time?"

Rural Survival Rules (Please)

Readers who have yet to be totally initiated into the rural routes would be wise to quickly learn some of the important rules for rural life.

Perhaps it will be more difficult for people who as adults leave their urban and suburban homes to experience life in the countryside. Those people, after all, don't have brothers or sisters who are willing to provide the hard – and sometimes quite painful – lessons that are needed to best understand those helpful rules.

Most are backed with total common sense, but seem to require experience before the lessons are fully realized. All of the rules are self-enforced, and breaking them can only add to the potential damage of essential body parts and to the psyche.

The most important rule has to be to never urinate on an electric fence wire – otherwise known as the "don't pee on the hot wire" rule.

I won't totally admit to having ever been foolish enough to allow a certain older brother talk me into peeing on an electric wire. If I had done it, I could tell you that urine is, indeed, an excellent conductor of electricity and that an electrical charge can travel extremely quickly from the wire through the groin area and up to the ends of the hairs on your head.

Peeing on an electric fence wire can whip cowlicks into a young boy's haircut.

He who pees on an electric fence knows the feeling of having his teeth feel as though they'd been pushed from their roots, only to be slammed back in, as his jaw slams shut to start the teeth-grinding show of excruciating pain.

He who pees on an electric fence also learns that a human truly is able to fly; at least to unknowingly leap quite a long distance. I'll always wonder whether the flying/leaping ability results from the electrical charge pushing a young boy's body away from the wire, or if the boy who pees on the wire subconsciously leaps/flies away from the wire because electricity has just hit a spot where no electrical shock should ever be allowed.

Another rule involving the fencer tells us to never believe some of the most famous words ever uttered by an older brother: "Yeah, I turned the fencer off."

The "fencer is off" rule is often disregarded by younger brothers throughout the countryside who want to believe that their brother has, for once, really turned the fencer off before the younger brother starts work on the electric fence or cow trainer.

The failure to heed the "fencer is off" rule results in a shock that jolts the younger brothers' senses and knocks them to the ground, similar to the way urinating on the electrical wire shocks younger brothers and knocks them to the ground. However, the "fencer is off" rule isn't nearly as painful as the "don't pee on the hot wire" rule is – umm, at least that's what I would imagine if anyone would be so foolish as to allow his brother to talk him into peeing on the fence.

Another important rule is the "don't run across the farmyard if you're hurt" rule. Those who are injured by a large piece of machinery falling onto one of their limbs should know better than to run, yelling, across the yard toward the house to seek a ride to old Doc Hable to get their gashed leg sewn back together. Somewhere in that yard, they should know, is an older brother who is lying in wait to tackle them to the ground and slap them until they yell louder and louder, until there is no breath left to yell – which we all know is a good way for an older brother to get control of a situation.

Again, the "don't run across the farmyard if you're hurt" rule can quickly result in a younger brother finding himself on the ground. However, the younger brother is likely to prefer the pain of a 50-stitch gash in his leg, and the slapped-until-subdued method, over the pain of having peed on an electric fence wire.

Another is the "find a responsible adult or qualified medical professional" rule, especially in matters such as in the healing of a deeply cut finger. If that rule is broken, it could result in providing a chance for an older brother to dispense quack-like medical advice; i.e. "if you stick that cut finger into that bag of cattle salt, the iodized salt will stop the bleeding and heal it faster." Those country people who have ever done anything like stick a cut finger into a bag of iodized cattle salt know the searing pain that might make the victim run, yelling, from the farm's granary and into the barn to seek the nearest water – only to have his father crack him alongside the head for being so loud and interrupting the evening's barn chores. It should be noted, of course, that none of those would be nearly as damaging to a child than having peed on the electric fence wire.

Among the rules, too many to mention in one chapter of a book, is the "bet you can't get there faster than me" rule.

Younger brothers are apt to break that rule by allowing an older brother to talk them into seeing who can be the first to reach a chore site. Winning such a challenge (the only time the younger brother manages to win a footrace with the older brother) usually means getting to do more of the chores than the older brother. The "bet you can't get there faster than me" rule can't compare with breaking the "don't pee on the hot wire" rule.

Learning all the rules for living on a rural route takes time – often upwards of 18 years.

The important thing to remember is, if one of the rules is broken, the lesson learned from the agony should be enough to assure that the rule is never broken a second time. As I've been told, that's especially important to remember if you've ever been talked into urinating on an electric fence wire.

Fighting the Forces of Gravity

I can't fly.

I know that to be fact; I've tried.

The attempt to fly was just one of the many results of an accident waiting to happen. The word "accident" could easily be interchanged with the names of a half-dozen boys in rural Veefkind. Throw in a few relatives from within a short drive and some might think we're lucky to be alive.

In Veefkind we tried to fly, blew things up, raced, had farm accidents, and had battles that involved some high-powered homemade weapons.

We all survived.

In our part of the world, few my age had new bicycles. Most of us had bicycles that were handed down from a previous generation, purchased at a thrift sale or – at the very best – handed down to us from brothers or sisters that were much older than us. In some cases, we actually created a new bicycle from parts of other bicycles.

That creation of a new bike was exactly what we did with my first one, a 24-inch unit that had parts from at least three other bicycles.

The fact that we didn't have new bikes didn't stop us from the most fun that could be imagined on bicycles. We had drag races on the gravel of Veefkind Road. There were short-track races around our farm's circular driveway. There were bicycle hill-climbing contests on farms' barn hills.

And then there was the flying.

Flying involved a small, wooden ramp made with a two-foot piece of two-by-six inch wood. It was attached to a wooden six-by-six inch block of wood with another block stacked on top of that.

The idea was simple: Pick up as much speed as we could in about 75 yards of gravel driveway, hit the ramp and soar as high and as far as we could. It was ski-jumping on bicycles; though we knew style points would mean only safe landings and being ready for a try at flying farther than the other guys.

I had plenty of practice, because the ramp was at our farm. It would be a debate for the other Veefkind guys to take up, but I'd argue that my 24-inch bike built from cannibalized bikes would fly with the best of them.

My cousin, Larry, stayed over for a few days one summer, and I made it a point to show him how far that bike really could soar. I made the run to the ramp and hit it with as much speed as I'd ever gathered. I flew – soared – as the bike left the ramp. The moment was held in slow motion as I and my trusty cycle defied gravity.

And it was in slow motion that I looked down to see the wheel fall from the bicycle's front forks. It went ahead without the rest of the bicycle and me, giving me a brief moment to comprehend how much the next few minutes might hurt.

The slow-motion effect ended as the bared forks touched the driveway's gravel. In a quick moment, they pierced into the gravel, stopping the front of the bike. The rest of the bike and I continued on, over the top of the forks, quickly flipping over and driving me face-first into the gravel.

"Larry, go tell Ma to call the ambulance," I managed to spit through a mouthful of gravel and a head full of ringing bells.

Roaming the Roads of Rural Life

Through the gravel that seemed to be packed into my head, I fully expected a trip to see old Doc Hable and even maybe a trip to a big-town hospital emergency room.

Larry, a witness to the carnage, did as I asked. He didn't know at first whether his cousin would survive. But, cooler – and clearer – heads than mine prevailed and an ambulance wasn't called. All I needed was some ice, some recovery time and a 9/16ths wrench to make sure the wheel's nuts were well-tightened before I tried that stunt again.

I survived the attempts to fly enough times to continue the neighborhood guys' escapades at the local township dump, which was a little more than a mile from our farm. We found many amusements there, including collecting as many aerosol cans as possible, then dumping them into a 55-gallon drum in which a fire had been started.

We knew enough to run as fast and as far from the barrel as possible. In seconds, the pressure-packed cans were exploding with a thunder that could be heard beyond our farm and sending ruptured cans high into the air.

We survived every junkyard visit.

Farm accidents were a bit more serious, but we somehow managed to live through them, too. A fellow named Terry, who had left Veefkind with his family to live in a city about an hour away, managed to be involved in two of them.

In one accident, Terry and my brother, Ed, loaded a hay wagon as I drove the tractor pulling our baler. The load wagon was nearing capacity, so Terry climbed to the top of the bales – seven or eight feet from the wagon's floor and about 12 feet from the ground. I glanced back to the wagon shortly after Terry had made that climb and realized that he was gone.

I stopped the tractor. When we checked behind the wagon, we found that about 40 bales had fallen from the back of the wagon, taking Terry to the ground with them. The three of us were amazed that he was uninjured.

Another accident involving Terry occurred when he and I were removing moldy waste from the top of a tower silo filled with corn silage. Machinery moved the silage from the silo to our emptied barn. It was our mission to use forks to throw it into a spreader. We both became quite ill from the gases, an illness that took us a few days to overcome. Old Doc Hable was right when he said we'd suffer for a few days but that we'd eventually feel better again.

We survived to join apple fights that were powered by some of the most massive homemade weapons ever brought to bear on humans and structures. Bicycle tire inner-tubes stretched between the large crotches of trees – or even between two trees – easily could launch green apples a couple hundred yards, and make them hit their targets with substantial force.

We survived a myriad of pranks, falls and accidents that left some of us with a few scars and maybe one or two slight deformities.

I survived, but with little urge to learn how to fly. Flying, as I learned in Veefkind, probably should be left to the birds and people in airplanes.

A License to Rubberneck

There wasn't any use in even giving the slightest toot of the horn to get the attention of the older fellow as he dilly-dallied down the road. It would have been a means of stopping the side-to-side swivel his head was making as he checked on every field and every neighborhood yard as he drove along at eight miles slower than the posted 55 miles per hour speed limit. But it also may have given him enough of a start to make him swerve into the ditch on either side of the narrow road.

His was country driving at its finest – nearly an artistic form of transportation along most rural routes.

Rural driving, I've found, takes many years to master. The older fellow had served his time; I figured he deserved the right to do all the neighborhood rubbernecking that he could muster at his age. The only thing impeding his efforts would be the limits of side-to-side flexibility in his neck, and his ability to assure that his car could stay in a single lane.

A fellow such as he probably wouldn't dream of driving on the streets of any metropolitan area's downtown. Chances are that he wouldn't even care to drive in the traffic of the city of 1,300 people, where for so many years he and his wife made a weekly Friday trip for groceries, haircuts, shoes and clothing.

He'd be the first to be critical of any young whipper-snapper with whom he'd ride in a car, too.

"You'd better start making complete stops at those stop signs, or you're gonna get a ticket."

"You'd better idle this baby down; I know the cop is around here off and on."

"I'm going to have to drive this thing for you sometime. I can handle 'er while I get it going so the carbon gets burned out."

"You going to kiss the ass of that car in front of us?"

"Geezuz, ya got less than a half-tank of gas in this thing. Why do you always have to be running on empty when I'm riding with you?"

It's best to just sit and give nods of agreement when listening to an old driver of rural routes. Certainly, glancing over at the guy in the peanut gallery is out of the question.

"Quit gawking around! Cripes; trying to run us off the road!?"

It doesn't matter how the old fellow drives. It doesn't matter that he drives the rural routes too slowly for the rest of the roads' traffic; it doesn't matter that he gawks and swerves down the road so much that his car's tracks look like sidewinder snakes had been racing down the road.

He'd paid his driving dues.

Just as that older man, I've worked hard on paying my driving dues along the rural routes. And, as with him, paying those dues started for me at a young age – a very, very young age.

Many of the rural guys in my generation drove their first powered vehicle sometime around their fifth or sixth birthday. I'm not talking about a riding lawn mower here either (indeed, I even chuckle to myself each time a city-born guy refers to his riding lawn mower as his "tractor"). I'm referring to a real tractor – in my case a Farmall Super M tractor.

I was perched in all my glory on the seat of our family's Super M the summer between my fifth and sixth birthday. I couldn't reach the pedals, which didn't matter; I hadn't yet acquired the power to be able to push them. I couldn't really turn the steering wheel much, as the Super M didn't have power steering, which didn't matter; there wasn't much steering that had to be done.

That first drive was made while our family was performing the unenviable chore of picking rocks from one of our farm's fields. The tractor was put in low gear and the throttle was set at a very low idle. The machine was barely moving and I was instructed to touch nothing besides the steering wheel and do no more driving than to hold the tractor in a relatively straight line as everyone else threw rocks onto the wagon being pulled by the tractor.

It wasn't long before I graduated to our small Ford tractor. Early into my sixth year, I'd mastered much about that tractor, which was much smaller than the Super M. The Ford was designed with the clutch and brake pedals in a fashion that allowed me to stand and reach them.

Whether I actually had the Ford mastered occasionally came into question. One of those times, Dad was leaving for a bit to buy some machinery parts and had instructed me to check the water tank that was filling in our heifer barn, across the spur railroad line that went through our yard and then across Veefkind Road from the home farm. The barn was all of 250 yards from our house, but I thought it important to drive the Ford tractor to complete my chore.

On the way back from the barn, I re-crossed Veefkind Road and approached the spot where the railroad crossed our driveway. Out of nowhere, there appeared a railroad work-unit approaching the crossing.

I stood hard on the tractor's brakes, but my six-year-old body didn't have the mass to push them enough to stop the tractor. I'd thrown it out of gear, but it seemed destined to roll into the railroad machinery that was crossing in front of me.

Challenging times sometimes make for creative actions. My creative action was to leap from the still-rolling tractor, run behind it and latch onto its drawbar. I gripped it as hard as I could, gritted my teeth and dug my heels into the driveway's gravel. Unbelievably, and much to my relief, I got the tractor stopped – but wondered whether I would have been better off having run into the railroad machine as I looked through teary sweat to see a dozen railroad workers nearly falling from their equipment as they roared with laughter.

Even with such a humiliating driving experience, I forged on with the rural drivers' education program. Within a couple of years, I'd mastered some minor fieldwork on that Ford tractor. And, soon after reaching the point of being able to see over the dashboard of our 1949 Ford pickup truck, I was using the truck to assist with occasional trips to fields hauling fencing materials or oats.

Driving the truck was itself an adventure. It wasn't the class of farm trucks; I'd never known it to be licensed or to have a muffler. Its double-range four-on-the-floor transmission created a young boy's visions of driving anything from an 18-wheeler to an Indy racing car. Clutch, shift, accelerate; clutch, shift, accelerate. Double-clutch when necessary. Let the engine compression do some of the braking, especially when the truck – which my entire life had been referred to as "The Old Truck" – sometimes had some air in its brake line and could occasionally be a challenge to stop.

A couple of pumps on the brake, even when there was some air in those brake lines, generally was enough to assure that it would stop.

Then, I turned 12.

It was at about that age when my brother, Ed, got his second motorcycle – a sleek red and chrome Yamaha street bike with an amazing (at least to a 12-year-old farm kid who was tired of riding his home-built bicycle) 180 cubic centimeter powerhouse. Fortunately, the brother of my life-long friend, Ken, also had a motorcycle of about the same size. Ken and I snuck those motorcycles out of our yards as often as we could for rides around Veefkind's graveled rural routes.

The fun ended, at least for a while, soon after a meeting of the minds between Ken and me late one afternoon at the west end of a two-mile stretch of Veefkind Road. As we relaxed on the seats of our brothers' motorcycles, we wondered which machine could beat the other to the county highway at the other end of the two miles.

The race was on.

Gravel flew behind us as we headed east. The speedometer on the cycle I was driving jumped to life as quickly as the rear tire could catch enough gravel beneath it to move me and the bike down the road. The speedometer needle had long-since crossed the "80" on its dial as I heard a quick "tuk-tuk" beneath me – the sound of the cycle's tires hitting the railroad crossing on Veefkind

Road a few yards west of our farmyard. I knew not to glance into our farmyard; that any deviation from my attention to the road could be disastrous.

We hadn't quite reached the highway when we hit a patch of loose gravel, bringing both of us to the realization that we needed to slow down before we were dumped from the motorcycles.

As we drove back to the west, I thought about the vision I thought I'd caught out of the corner of my eye as we passed the farm.

Dad, for some reason, happened to have been in the yard and witnessed the near-suicidal race of a couple of pre-teens. I wondered later how the pain of being dumped from a speeding motorcycle would have compared with the consequences that I faced as I made the lonely drive into the yard.

Ironically, it was Ken who also joined me in our first state-legalized driving expedition. He and I made our first over-the-road drivers' education trip with our driving teacher, who also was my high school football coach. I took the wheel first, driving out of our little town on the two-lane state highway that doubles as the community's Main Street.

As we got a few miles out of town, Coach brought to light the real drivers' education programs available to so many rural boys.

"I always like riding with the farm boys in drivers' education," Coach said. "Most of 'em been drivin' since they were six."

Coach gave me a knowing glance as I negotiated the drivers' education car around a curve.

"Only thing," Coach added, "when ya drive with me, ya gotta take your elbow back in from the window and remember to keep both hands on the wheel, or you're never gonna pass your drivers' test. And while you're at it, ya don't haveta wave at everybody we meet – and quit lookin' at those fields!"

There would be many chances, I knew even then, for me to take those casual drives down the road to check out what's happening in the countryside – who's got their haying started and who still has some corn to plant.

Hopefully, nobody will startle me by blowing their horn. I believe, after all, that I will have earned my license to be yet another old rubbernecker of the rural routes.

Slips of the Knife

The pocket knife was nowhere to be found, and it added to the numbness that chilled the cramped room. Any other time, we might have laughed about it. But just then wasn't the time for any laughter.

Dad lay still in the bed, the life gone from his body. He'd drawn his last breath less than an hour earlier and couldn't offer the good-natured arguments or accusations about the disappearance of his knife as he might have a month or two earlier. Eighty-six years had drained the life from his body, and he'd disappeared from this world just as his pocket knife had disappeared from that room.

We knew he was going to be gone. We didn't know his pocket knife would be gone.

I fully doubt many of the health care professionals in that building would have understood what was so important about that knife, unless their ties were truly of a rural nature; making questions about the whereabouts of such a seemingly meaningless tool seem trivial.

Generation after generation of rural boys watched with longing as knives were pulled from their fathers' pockets and unfolded to perform some near act of magic. The blade might perform the minor surgery of removing a sliver from a child's finger. It might cut the strings of bales to hasten the job of feeding heifers. It might trim the hair of a cow's tail. It might halve an apple to share it with a friend. It might field-dress the harvest of a small-game hunt. It might cut an extra notch into a belt or harness.

The knife was to be treated with honor. The only time it left a father's pocket for anything but work was when it was moved from one pair of pants to another.

Little boys could only hope the day would soon come when the honor of having their own knives would be reality.

The reality of having my own knife came much sooner than when most town folks would be willing to allow a son to carry a knife in his pocket.

When I was six, getting that first knife made me feel like one of the neighborhood men. It made me feel that I could be capable of doing the type of work that was made for grown men.

Unfortunately, my pocket knives couldn't seem to stay in my pocket. I'm quite sure mine were equipped with tiny legs that helped it crawl out of my pockets. And there definitely was a magnetic draw in the hay. A Saturday afternoon of play in the haymow meant the knife's disappearance.

Strange thing about that haymow, too: Once a knife was lost in it, the knife was gone forever. Searches of every stem of hay have never turned up a single knife lost in the haymow, making me believe the hay had qualities that could dissolve such an object.

I didn't need anyone to tell me that I was cursed to never be able to maintain ownership of a pocket knife for a very long time – at least the ones I'd intended to carry within my pocket for any extended time. For me, the only way to hold continuous ownership of a pocket knife seemed to be handing it to a friend to have the knife locked away in a safe-deposit box.

Though I didn't need any reminder of those facts, Dad had ample opportunity to offer his opinion on the issue.

He sometimes had good reason.

Never being able to hang onto my own knife, it naturally followed that I never had one with me when he and I worked together on a project. That would bring me to utter the words he never wanted to hear: "Let me borrow your knife."

The first one or two times were the mistakes of a teenager, I suppose. I'd finished cutting hay that had been twisted on the shaft of a piece of machinery and, without much thought, folded the knife and slipped it into my pocket. A day or two later, he'd remind me that I'd used his knife and a quick check of my pockets would make his knife reappear.

As we aged, the routine turned into a game. The time between the two of us working on a project became more sporadic. When they did occur, the hope that it would involve needing to borrow Dad's pocket knife always was in the back of my mind.

The work would start.

"Hey, Dad, I need a knife. Got one on you?"

His hand would slip into one of his pockets, and then stop as his attention was drawn directly to me.

"Make sure I get it back."

My hand would dart toward him and make a beckoning motion.

"C'mon, I need it now!"

He would reluctantly hand it to me and we'd continue the work. I'm pretty sure he noticed every time that I'd try to draw his attention to something else about the project and then fold the borrowed knife and slip it into my jeans.

Some time would pass – maybe just a few seconds, maybe an hour; he might have waited until we sat together for lunch. His words would come when he hoped I'd least expect them.

"Did you forget something? Maybe you should reach into that pocket and give my knife back."

I'd hand the knife back. He'd tell me he had to remember to never let me borrow his knife again, because he was pretty sure that a couple of his disappeared at my hands. I'd tell him I'm sure this was the first time I'd ever borrowed his knife, and if it wasn't, I'm sure I'd never forgotten to return it.

If any truth was ingrained into me, it was that there were a couple of tools that you don't want to have to ask a farmer to borrow; and if you do, you'd better hand it right back: pliers and pocket knives.

Many farmers carry pliers in a holster just as an Old West gunslinger would tote his sidearm. Knives are hidden in jeans' pockets and – more recently – in leather belt cases similar to those that hold the pliers. The tools are wielded with the skill of an artist, whipped from their compartments and used to slash and squeeze the way to a job's completion.

In a farmer's eyes, tools such as those can be much more than just tools. They're crutches. They're job-savers. They're friends.

The most impressive ones to me are those tools, especially the pocket knives, which have been maintained for many years. They're the ones which have been worn smooth from wear; any printing that had been on the sides is long gone, if the side covers are left at all. Chances are that an aging pocket knife has one side with flat, exposed steel where a black or white plastic handle once had been attached. Blades had been sharpened and re-sharpened until their sharp steel was a third of their original size.

The knife that should have been inside a drawer in that room the day my father moved into another phase of life was one of those long-treasured tools. Like him, it was worn; the years of work and exposure to the environment had long-sapped the strength that held its pieces together.

Where the knife went remains a mystery. In his final days, we'd watched as painkilling drugs took control of Dad's mind. He lay in his bed, hallucinations overtaking his earthly reality, and we watched as his hands made motions of work from long past; as he ordered us to hook up teams of workhorses that he'd owned a half-century earlier. Chances are, those hallucinations took him to times when he needed to pull a knife from his pocket so a project could be completed – maybe even loaning the knife to his youngest son with one of those reminders to return it.

We could spend plenty of time wondering where his last pocket knife really went.

I hope he stuck it into his pocket and remembered to take it with him.

The War of Birds

I estimated there to be about 25 pigeons in the small flock that swooped in front of my truck as I drove down a rural road.

It was the middle of January, so I surmised that the pigeons simply were making their sporadic pigeon-like flight from feeding in the stubble of the picked corn field on the left side of the road or on the cow manure that had been spread that morning on the field on the right. It's always a bit challenging to tell exactly where country pigeons have been – or, for that matter, where they are going.

Country pigeons are nothing like city pigeons. Unlike city pigeons, the country birds shy away from humans. In the country, pigeons don't gather around park benches to munch on seeds thrown by people of leisure. Instead, the pigeons are on their own to feed on corn and oats left behind by pickers and combines; they seek undigested seeds in animal waste. Country pigeons flitter in and out of farmyards to find spilled feed in front of granaries and inside silos. They sneak into the nooks and crannies of

Rural Routes & Ruts

barns and machine sheds, making nests in the crooks of the buildings' rafters.

Country pigeons are a nuisance. They leave disease-laden waste wherever they go, wherever they perch. Cattle don't care to eat the hay and silage that's been covered with pigeon waste.

In many ways, pigeons are similar to starlings in their filth – except that a farm cat will at least eat a pigeon, while turning a nose up to a starling.

For all the aforementioned reasons, it became the duty of young teenagers from Veefkind to try to rid the neighborhood of pigeons. Our mission was simple: Find as many ways as possible to make cat food out of the birds.

Some people worry about the potential war of the worlds. Ours was a war of the birds.

The battles took on many forms during our developmental years.

The wars started when we were far too young to be fighting such battles the way we were fighting them (by more modern standards, I'm pretty certain someone would go to jail for allowing their children to do things as they were done a few years back).

Acrobatics and BB guns were the primary tools of those early battles. The BB guns had just enough power to reach from haymow floors to pigeons that sat on old hay-fork rails and rafters in our barns, and when well-aimed, enough to make a mortal hit on the birds.

The acrobatics were much more adventurous than the use of the BB guns. Not exceedingly acrobatic, my role in that method was limited. A couple of the guys, however, were able to climb – in some spots upside down – up rafters to surprise pigeons or to destroy nests high above the haymow floor.

Acrobatics weren't confined to the heights of the barn. A legendary case-in-point was when a mortally wounded pigeon fell to the cover of a hay chute. One of my cousins – a town boy but an honorary Veefkind boy – didn't heed our warnings and leapt into the chute from about 10 feet of bales that surrounded it. As he made the leap, I had an immediate vision of what the results would be, and moments later my vision was confirmed. The leaper crashed through the chute cover and was found lying on his back in a pigpen, covered with pig manure and pigs sniffing around him, another eight feet below the chute cover.

My cousin survived the ordeal and years later the memory served as a moment of laughter between us during the sad occasion of his father's wake.

We advanced to real firearms as we reached our teenage years. Shotguns of several gauges completed our arsenal, which was used to ambush the birds from all angles on the farms. It took great coordination to chase the birds from barn to barn and even from farm to farm. The assignment for some hunters was to chase pigeons from the barns or silos so shooters outside the buildings could make their shots.

Those who see the shotgunning as being a slaughter should realize that a pigeon-shoot is no chicken-shoot. The picture of fat bench-fed park pigeons is nothing like the reality of the darting and dodging of wary country pigeons.

The pigeons neared their ultimate victory one late-winter afternoon when I joined two of the Veefkind boys on snowmobiles to shoot pigeons in fields where manure was spread. With shotguns lain across our laps, we worked a system of riding the snowmobiles in a formation that would surround the birds from three sides, which was proving to be amazingly effective. The birds would leap from their feast as we approached and, if our circle had tightened enough, they were apt to fly over one of us and that lucky gunner would have the chance to create winter scavenger food.

Unfortunately for me, the excitement of the moment caused great harm. Riding my brother's new snowmobile, I was bounding from one rock-hard snowdrift to another when the sled's skis stuck into one drift.

It sent the snowmobile rolling end-for-end several times over, and left me lying on top of an old Stevens single-shot 12-gauge shotgun. As I lay there, I hoped with all my might that I'd only knocked the wind out of me, and that I hadn't forgotten to unload the shotgun and taken a load of birdshot point-blank in the abdomen.

With much trepidation, I pulled one of my hands from beneath me to check for blood. Though still trying to catch my breath, I rejoiced that I wouldn't be known as the goofball who left his innards all over a field of manure in Veefkind.

As I recovered, I looked up to appraise what had happened to the snowmobile. When I saw that the snowmobile's hood had been demolished, and that its handlebars were at a 90-degree angle from where they should have been, I considered whether I would have been better off having taken the load of shot in the guts. I knew the thumping that I would receive from that brother – a fear that came to fruition.

The clean up of neighborhood pigeons came to an end as we reached the end of our high school years. We went our own ways to fight our own wars.

Sometimes, when we've gathered in later years, the boys from Veefkind have talked about those times of trying to control the area's pigeon population. We've talked about what we could have done to make our efforts more effective, what we could have done to turn us into bird-ridding heroes in the neighborhood farmers' eyes.

As with so many of the things that mixed the Veefkind boys' youthful energy, creative strategies, fun and serious work, I'm betting we learned some lessons in those miniature wars with the birds.

Those lessons certainly include seeing to it that we'd do our best to assure that our children and grandchildren not take many of the youthful risks that we'd taken. I hope we're only partly successful in that endeavor, because I want future generations to live and gain experience-rich lessons afforded us.

I often hope that my now-grown children have their own flocks of pigeons that will remind them of youthful lessons learned – including even the important ones like not jumping onto a barn chute cover or not driving a snowmobile with a shotgun lying across your lap.

Hopefully, my children and their children will have more success with their wars with birds.

Finding the Way to the Target

The deer stood about 300 yards away – too far to determine with my bare eye whether it had the horns to make it a legal buck. I turned up the power on my rifle's scope and, seeing that it indeed was a deer legal for me to harvest, pulled the trigger. The deer fell, dead, a second or two after I'd felt my rifle's recoil slamming into my shoulder.

The deer had been part of one of the most successful deer hunting mornings for my family. Every condition had been right that morning, and all family members in our hunting party had harvested legal bucks.

Every hunter among us had shot well, a fact that in many circles should have quelled debates about who in a family is the "best shot." But that's not the way it is along many rural routes – once the back-slapping and congratulating gets done and the stories of the hunt end, chances are good that someone in my family is bound to say something like, "good thing it was me doing the shooting, because I doubt you could make a shot like that."

That's the way the morning of our perfect hunt had ended. We were three brothers in a minor debate over whether a harvested deer had been 50 yards away or 160 yards away, and which of the three of us actually had dropped the trophy buck at which all three of us had shot at the same time.

Many of the challenging boasts seem to be directed at me, the only one of my father's sons who had been professionally trained in marksmanship while in the U.S. Marine Corps. No matter which direction the debates took, though, all three of his sons – me included – could hold our own in taking verbal shots at each other and taking rifle shots at wild game.

Sometimes, the debates get as deep as making claims on being the best-ever shooter in our family. That's when the debate ends.

The best ever, we know, isn't any of the three of us. It wasn't my father, either, or my grandfathers or any other guys whose genes we share.

The best shooter ever, we know, was my father's mother – Grandma Ida.

The "mighty hunters" that the men in my family ever have claimed to be paled in comparison with the marksmanship Grandma could level from the back porch of the house she shared with Grandpa. She didn't bring home much for wild game, but we knew no unwanted creatures were safe once she loaded her trusty Stevens single-shot .22 caliber rifle.

Skunks, nuisance birds, gophers, packs of wild dogs – they and others like them could kiss their tails goodbye once Grandma decided to place her rifle's front-sight bead into the "v" of its rear sight. And, though we were sure she didn't find Grandpa to be such a pest to have around, even he wasn't always safe from the wrath of Grandma's rifle.

Nobody in my generation is really certain of exactly how Grandma got to be such an expert marksman, but by the way she could knock a small bird off a telephone wire at 100 yards, we suspect she may have honed her shooting skills by using her bullets from her rifle to drive 10-penny nails into posts 200 yards away.

We truly know of Grandma's toughness, the greatest evidence being the shortened pinky finger on one of her hands. She lost part of that finger as a child when her brother dared her to lay her hand onto the block her parents used for chopping off chickens' heads in preparation for butchering. Her brother raised the chicken-chopping hatchet and dared her to keep her hand there so he could chop off her finger – fully believing she would pull it away before he lowered the hatchet. Grandma left her hand on the block, fully believing her brother wouldn't have the audacity to slam the sharp hatchet onto the block.

The chopping-block incident grows in family lore as we've wondered how they explained to their parents why young Ida was suddenly missing part of one of her digits.

Later in her life, creatures that didn't belong around Grandpa and Grandma's yard were making a fatal mistake by entering it. The nasty critters' lives were yesterday's news once Grandma grabbed that rifle. She would open its bolt and slip one of her small, brass cartridges into the rifle's chamber, then close the bolt and crack open the house's back door. Grandma would prepare for her deadly shot with only a few inches of the rifle's barrel stuck out of the doorway, pulling back the rifle action's cocking knob just before taking aim on her quarry.

"Pow!"

The crisp, firecracker-like sound of the rifle would momentarily echo in the house as Grandma completed her deed. She ejected the empty shell casing from the rifle as she pulled it back into the house to lean it near the door in preparation for the next time she'd require its services.

Seldom did the unwanted creatures escape the yard before Grandma was able to touch off one of her deadly shots. If they did, Grandma would uncock the rifle – a tricky process for that type of gun, having to hold the cocking knob while the trigger is pulled, then easing the knob forward so the action's hammer could no longer snap forward into its firing pin. The unfired cartridge then would be removed from the rifle's chamber.

One time, Grandma's fingers slipped from the cocking knob as she was unloading the rifle. Grandma had already turned, facing into the house, meaning the rifle's muzzle was pointed into her kitchen.

"Pow!"

From his perch atop the toilet stool in their bathroom, Grandpa heard the rifle shot as he had hundreds of times before. That time, however, he was surprised to hear the popping noise continue in the bathroom – the noise caused by a .22 caliber bullet snapping through the wooden bathroom door and whizzing past his face before lodging into the bathroom wall.

The bullet had zinged into their kitchen, ricocheted off the tile floor, then into the kitchen wall before ricocheting back across the kitchen, where it did its deed in the bathroom. It's been wholeheartedly agreed in the family that Grandpa was at least sitting in the right spot to have come so close to meeting his fate a few years too early.

Her near-miss aside, I only wish Grandma would have been around long enough to have had some laughs about her grandsons' marksmanship debates.

It's easy to believe we'd have enjoyed trying to prove ourselves to her – and to our other grandparents, for that matter. None of them would have necessarily needed us to prove ourselves to them; we know that for fact, having ourselves become parents and grandparents.

And, whatever the truth in our marksmanship debates, it's comforting to feel someone like Grandma in me when I'm trying to do something as intricate as hitting a small target over great distances.

I remember lying on my belly on a Marine Corps rifle range, wondering how I could possibly guide a bullet so true over the 500 yards to its target. It took a few shots before I realized that Grandma's spirit was somewhere out there on the range, using her strong hands – short pinky finger and all – to guide the bullets to their targets.

She was there with me that day, guiding my bullet true over the hundreds of yards to the deer I harvested the morning of her grandsons' most successful hunting morning.

It's that way with our ancestors, I believe. They never leave us; though we may not see them here to share our laughs, tears, trials and triumphs, they're forever in us and guiding us to our targets.

Company on a Country Walk

I stopped to visit my mother's grave out at Veefkind the other day. I felt a presence with me as I stood under the shade of the pine trees that hang over her handpicked lot.

I felt the warmth of knowing my big sister, LaVonne, was there with me to visit with Mom.

It was a feeling like none I'd had since Vonnie's departure from this early stage of our lives. It was a feeling that's helped me put my selfish worldly mind at ease about her going from her mortal being to her eternal being.

Vonnie, always the big sister, was there to offer the knowledge that, like Mom, she is happy and comfortable in her new stage of life. She joined me as I criss-crossed the small, well-groomed cemetery to take note of several generations of the paternal side of my family.

It was a walk together for which we were long overdue; one that, while unexpected, brought me great satisfaction. So many of us had known Vonnie as a special sort of giver. Sure, as her pastor so aptly pointed out at her funeral, she could dart her quick "I know" glance that could put even the most hard-hearted of us in our place – a glance which always was joined with a little smile formed at the corner of her mouth. Her expressions left us wondering whether that smile said "I won" or "I'm just having fun with you."

Vonnie was special because her giving stretched across the rural countryside from central Iowa to central Wisconsin. That was a lot of giving.

Now, we can beat ourselves up plenty for not having said "thank you" to a person like Vonnie for all the giving she'd provided; for those times she'd made people smile at our little one-room school or at a get-together of Veefkind neighborhood friends. But, I don't think we have to beat ourselves up that way; the mother in her said the only thanks needed was our acceptance of her giving.

Still, there is only so much giving that can be done by one human being. The miles, the number of people she touched, made it impossible for her to be with all of us as much as she or any of us would have liked. We all understood that, I think, and happily accepted the times that she could spend with any of us; the time that she could be "giving" to us as friends and family; the time that she could make us laugh or cry with stories of friendship and family love.

Like so many of us, I felt the selfish anger that goes with grief when Vonnie left. Grandparents die. Even parents die. We know that. But, sisters and brothers – especially those still young – aren't supposed to die. Or, more troubling from our father's perspective, children aren't supposed to die before their parents.

Our faith makes us understand that Vonnie reached the goal we're all seeking. We find comfort in that – perhaps not immediately, but as time passes, it becomes more comforting.

I've fallen back on that comfort of faith with so many losses in my life. I've used my faith to heal. And, as importantly, I've used the comfort of the rural countryside to heal me.

The departure of loved ones has left emptiness in my heart. I long for their laughter; I long even for their admonishments and for the silly games of keeping them guessing about which goofy thing I could be getting ready to say next.

I've managed to make some deals with God during my time spent on a rural stump, contemplating a loss like Vonnie.

In the bargain, we get to have more of someone like Vonnie than was ever possible while she walked the earth with us. No, we won't be able to see her as she laughs with us about the silly things she did while growing up with her five brothers and sisters. We won't see her as she reminisces about the special friendships that helped her grow as a person. We won't see her lips tighten as she banters with her husband. We won't have her arms wrapped around us with hugs or see and hear what she's done to help her children and grandchildren.

Instead, Vonnie – the giver – is able to offer her love, her big-sisterly guidance, to us in a much deeper and caring fashion than she ever was able to in her brief time on earth. She's able to always reach us through the piece of her that God placed into every heart she ever touched.

The grief I've felt through losses of loved people like Vonnie has taught me much about the empty space they leave in our hearts. The most earthly comfort we can find, I think, is the knowledge that our hearts are built with two chambers. One chamber will be pumped empty at a given moment, but the other side will always be full.

Vonnie walked with me as never before as she and I left Veefkind – together – that day, just as she now walks with all of us through every moment of every day. I have her filling an area of my heart that's never before been filled.

The Lessons of Death's Gifts

Those who fully experience the rural routes know the excitement of living and the reality of death. My rural life gave me what I'd viewed as a rational understanding that, as we age, death will take some of the people close to us.

My father tried hard to make me understand death when, as a boy, I asked him about our animals' deaths and then about his own fear of dying. Even after the death of his father, Dad assured me there's nothing to fear about death.

Dad wasn't a philosopher. Dad was a dairy farmer.

Being a straight-forward talker in such matters, Dad told me he wasn't frightened about his own death – which would come about 40 years after I'd first asked about the issue. He explained that death is as much a part of living as birth; that there's really not much sense in taking valuable time to worry about such an inevitable matter.

His explanation may actually have been a little more to the point. Maybe he stopped for a moment during one of his trips down our barn's alley just long enough to say something like, "I miss your grandpa, but there's no use worrying about dying, 'cause it's going to happen to all of us; now, get the goddamned calves fed."

I understood his point.

As I've aged – I'm about the age Dad was when I originally asked him the questions – I've come to realize that he's right in believing there's no sense worrying about my own demise. As he aptly pointed out, death is going to get me at some time or another.

My farm upbringing and Dad's answers helped prepare me for what was to come, but it was difficult to deal with when family deaths started hitting me during the late 1990s. It wasn't long before I realized how I hadn't found answers to many "other" death questions. Dad's answers had touched the most basic questions, but seeing his reaction to his own personal losses – especially the deaths of his parents, my mother and my oldest sister – I don't think he could have found enough answers if he'd been granted 30 lifetimes.

Death comes fast and furious to a family of a person having passed his mid-life years. Since that time – and the death that goes with it – has come to me, I've felt like a prize fighter who's taken barrage after barrage of punches to my body, with an occasional uppercut landing on my chin hard enough to knock me to my knees.

It's nearly bearable when a year or more separates family losses. But some losses, I've found, come within months – even weeks – of each other.

Experience has taught me that death brings pain beyond description, but some comfort can be found in the lessons the deceased have taught me.

Sometimes, I'm finding those lessons to be easily felt.

After losing four men in my family – all of which occurred within two years – the lessons have been easy for me to understand.

When Dad died, my reflections made me realize how he best taught me without speaking. Most farm boys learn just by following their father around the farm and doing what their dad's doing, and I was no different.

When Dad did talk seriously, he did it in a way that was short and easy for me to understand. But being a person of words for most of my life, I learned in my teen years that I shouldn't question the form of language Dad used in any tense situation.

Dad sometimes talked with the back of his hand, with the flat part of his wide, leather belt or with a Surge milking machine strap. Sometimes he talked with a wry smile and a cocky, drooping of his eyelids.

Roaming the Roads of Rural Life

He challenged me by asking whether I thought I was capable of doing a job or beating an athletic opponent. He seldom cried, and when he did, it was easy to know that the pain was serious.

Above all, Dad taught me to be strong and to not back down for anyone or anything.

More lessons came with the loss of Bob, one of my brothers-in-law. Bob, who spent endless hours fishing on lakes throughout Wisconsin, died too young in a boating accident while fishing with an old friend.

In Bob, I saw a man who showed people like me that it's OK to be "me." As with anyone, Bob had dreams and goals; those about which I'd never asked, but which I'm certain were there. I'm not sure how many of them he accomplished or realized.

But, after his death, I realized how Bob's greatest deed may have been in "being Bob." Maybe he could have found ways to greater wealth and to more personal glory. Instead, his riches came in a happy family, the smiles he put on faces at his factory job, and in the time he spent fishing and hunting.

I got to spend time hunting with Bob and some limited time fishing with him. Maybe Bob would have liked to down a nice buck every year he hunted, but he didn't. He'd probably have liked to get his limit in partridge, ducks or geese during each hunt, but he didn't.

Bob was sincere about the camaraderie of the hunt being more important than any bag limit.

I'd heard criticism about the way he didn't seem to care whether members of his hunting party filled their deer tags; I'm sure he even heard some of it. But those criticisms, as with concerns over bag limits and other issues in his world, simply didn't seem to matter much.

What mattered was that he was true to himself; that he could wake in the mornings knowing all else would fall into place if he followed his own heart.

Bob strove to be only "Bob." He succeeded, and as I looked at his mortal remains lying in a coffin, I found comfort knowing he'd done well in that most important of personal challenges.

Lawrence lived the same long life as his younger brother, my father.

Uncle Lawrence was a spit-fire type who had the same stern ways as my father. Uncle Lawrence was our family's first all-conference high school football player and I worked hard to follow his legacy.

Into his 80s, Uncle Lawrence could be seen jumping in and out of a fishing boat or climbing the highest heights of a deer hunting stand.

One of my brothers, when questioning my need to take on a challenge such as a full marathon, often asked me "what, do you think your name is Lawrence?" I always took that as a high compliment.

As with my father, many could classify Uncle Lawrence with the moniker "bullheaded," although Uncle Lawrence's came packaged as a gallon of gasoline beside a lit match. I take pride in having learned that set-jaw tenacity – even though I don't think I ever could totally match that which he had – from Uncle Lawrence.

I've also learned from the loss of my mother's youngest brother, Jim.

Uncle Jim was a teacher. A few years ago, he called to ask me to spend a couple of hours addressing his high school students on the subject of leadership. I found some irony in that request, as I later thought about it, because I knew his students already had a great leader in front of them whenever Uncle Jim spoke. I took the challenge, but I felt humbled addressing the students in Uncle Jim's presence.

Uncle Jim showed me that it's OK to dream, and to find satisfaction in the pursuit rather than the outcome.

It seemed I'd spent much of my life trying to prove myself to people who called me their friend. That was never the case with Uncle Jim, who easily expressed to me his pride in what I'd accomplished.

Mother often told me I was much like Uncle Jim and called us her "absent-minded professors," because we might forget to comb our hair in the morning when our brains were working on stuff. I absorbed that with pride, because if there were men I wouldn't mind being compared to, he would be at the top of the list.

At Uncle Jim's wake, I saw students he'd taught and athletes he'd coached. It made me realize the "hidden teacher" within me. One teacher may forever change many lives because of a good word or a single attempt to direct a young person down the right road; efforts that might well be passed from that student to the student's children and grandchildren – and for generations to come.

Uncle Jim reminded me how good being a teacher can feel.

In reflection, I know – as I believe Dad knew that day in our barn 40 years ago – there's no escaping the pain and emptiness we feel when the people we love die. I also know, if we call a deceased person a "loved one," they will have taught us lessons if we open our hearts and minds to them.

Death's punches will continue to drop me to my knees every time I lose a loved one. But I'm better prepared to get up and fight again because I've allowed myself to learn the lessons of those who have gone before me. Those lessons are gifts that make me who I am.

Close Clips at Harry's and Mary's

I need a haircut, but I'm not sure where to go or exactly how to get it cut. There is this salon and that stylist; there is the scissors cut for a layered look and the clippers cut for a closely trimmed crew cut.

Something as simple as getting a haircut is nearly becoming a series of major decisions; it wasn't always that way for me. Getting a haircut used to be as simple as going to Harry's or Mary's.

In my early years, even the choice between Harry's and Mary's wasn't my decision – someone else made that choice for me.

Mary's wasn't even really a barbershop. It's the name of one of my three sisters, all of whom took turns cutting my hair. LaVonne, Mary and Rebecca – they all took their turns at trimming my follicles. I'm the youngest of six children. On occasion, I wondered whether I was born for my sisters' collective amusement.

With my arrival, there was little need for my parents to purchase dolls for the girls. They had me.

At that time, most all the guys had short-cropped tapered cuts, butches or crewcuts during the first 10 years of their lives. There were older guys who had ducktails or the like, but my folks were quick to point out how any hint of long hair was only good for "beatniks." Respectable guys had respectable haircuts.

Dad reiterated that point to no end that fateful Sunday night when four guys from England who called themselves "The Beatles" appeared on the Ed Sullivan Show.

The Beatles had bangs hanging an inch or so onto their foreheads, and by God and several other biblical figures rattled off in Dad's tirade, nobody in his house "had best show up wearing hair like that."

I flinched a bit as Dad said that. I'd already had some challenges at that shop I've come to call Mary's. Even as a first grader, there had been times when I'd rather have not shown up in school out of embarrassment for my latest haircut.

Still, I wonder, how can anyone so screw up a butch haircut that a first-grader wouldn't want to show his head in public?

It was because of my haircuts at Mary's that I learned one of my longstanding jokes:

Q: What's the difference between a good haircut and a bad haircut?

A: Two weeks and a stocking cap.

I often wore stocking caps, even during the hottest, muggiest dog days in July and August. I learned the versatility of the word "nick." Nick refers to sudden, unplanned and uneven smatterings of nearly shaved spots in my hair. Nick refers to the little red, bloody spots where there had been skin moments before the hair clipper started to buzz.

My sisters blamed my worst haircuts on the many cowlicks in my red mane.

I blamed their vision and unsteady hands.

Certainly, it taught me some character to risk my scalp to their teenaged hands. But, to this day, I can't understand how Marine Corps barbers could cut my hair so quickly and so closely – no nicks, no cuts, no errors – while my sisters never got it quite right.

Although I learned plenty during haircuts at Mary's, it was at Harry's where I got better haircuts and learned so much about family and the culture of our rural community.

But it wasn't having my hair cut that makes me most remember my days – and nights – at Harry's. Harry cut four generations of my family's hair, from my grandfather down to my son, Jamie.

Jamie's first haircut at Harry's reminded me of what's probably good about any rural town's barbershop.

That Friday night, a fishing show was playing on the portable television that Harry kept at the shop. There was a boy about 10 years old sitting in the big barber's chair as we waited for Jamie's turn. The boy was cringing each time Harry's electric clipper touched the back of his head, a fact not missed by Jamie, who was just short of 5 years old.

"Dad, I'm a little scared," Jamie whispered to me.

It wasn't as though Jamie was about to get his first haircut. Before that, he'd had his hair cut by people known as stylists in places known as beauty shops.

As I'd learned long before, Jamie learned that night that magazines like Outdoor Life and Sports Illustrated are the reading materials of choice at a shop like Harry's. Good Housekeeping and People magazines were found in the beauty shops.

He learned that pictures of beautiful women showing off new hairstyles hang on beauty shops' walls. Mounted fish hang on the walls of a place like Harry's.

As the fishing show progressed that night, I remembered sitting on my grandpa's lap just a few chairs away from the one in which Jamie sat. I remembered being there on many Friday nights with Dad and Grandpa, with a certain amount of fear in my heart that my ear might be accidentally severed when I got into the big barber's chair – undoubtedly a holdover feeling from my haircuts at Mary's.

Sitting in the barber's chair is a monumental affair for a young boy. It was the chair that everybody in the shop looked at while Harry worked on reducing the piles of protein on guys' heads.

The big barber's chair is center stage.

I looked around Harry's shop that night, and saw that very little had changed about it in the previous 25 years – yet another quality held by most rural barbershops. The fish might not have been the same one hanging over the big mirror on the shop's north wall – but it was a fish, all the same, and the place wouldn't have seemed the same without a fish there.

The magazine subscriptions seemed to be the same as they'd been for the previous 25 years, too, and for good reason: a picture of a big fish on the cover of some of the magazines probably sparked some of the greatest fishing stories ever told in a barbershop.

Grand fishing stories seem to fit well in barbershops like Harry's. It's the same with stories of fantastic deer hunts or with any general stories where a guy can comfortably spice them with slight fibs without fear of criticism.

Some of the old gang already wasn't able to get to Harry's that night. My favorite old-time visitor was Doc Hable, the local country doctor who had a knack for telling great hunting and fishing stories. He talked often about some mysterious hole in the Black River where he could always hook a musky or two.

Finally, it was Jamie's turn, his moment to be in the big chair at center stage.

He hopped onto the board used to elevate little guys in barber chairs and chatted with Harry while the barber expertly handled the psyche of a 5-year-old who isn't sure of what's coming next. Before he was done, Jamie was giggling with every tickle of Harry's scissors and clippers.

Harry's tools tried to make sense of the cowlicks on Jamie's head just as they had with cowlicks in the same spots on my head.

It was late for a business to be open on that night, and the area folk were no longer making their weekly small-town shopping trips on Friday nights like those. The place was empty by the time Jamie climbed down from the barber's chair.

I didn't bother to inspect Jamie's haircut; I simply paid Harry $4, knowing in my heart that he'd done the same good job of barbering that he'd done on Grandpa, Dad and me.

As we left though, Harry's buzzed with the Friday nights I'd spent there when I was Jamie's age.

Harry, meanwhile, swept around his chair, cleaning up hair from his fourth generation of customers.

Building Big Bridges

When I was a little boy, my mother often told me about this monstrous bridge that had been built. It was miles and miles long, she told me, and would link Michigan's Upper Peninsula with its Lower Peninsula.

I was a little young to realize the engineering and technology that must have been put into the bridge. I only knew from experience how a mile sure seemed like a long

Roaming the Roads of Rural Life

way – all the way from the Veefkind Church to the paved county trunk highway.

Determined, as always, to impress Mom, I boldly told her I someday would build a bridge to rival that one. Or, maybe I'd even build one that would go right across the heart of the great Lake Michigan and link Wisconsin and Michigan's Lower Peninsula so she wouldn't have to fly over or go around the lake to see her sister in Detroit.

Mom never stopped me from telling her I'd accomplish such a feat. That's a good thing about moms.

There may have been times when she stopped me from doing things that could bring physical pain to me or someone else. But, for the most part, she never stomped on any of my dreams.

She may have known my mathematical skills always would be a bit shaky, leading me down the road of struggle to just get through high school algebra, physics and geometry courses. She let me dream, even knowing I never had the workings of an engineer capable of building a house of cards, much less a large bridge.

It wasn't until recently that I started to understand why she may not have stopped my bridge-building dreams – which, in my youngest days, ranked as my greatest promise to her.

Needless to say, I never delivered on the promise of building that bridge, or any other bridge. Had I built it, I probably would have read about the feat in newspaper, instead of being the person writing about it.

In retrospect, however, I have been building much greater bridges – bridges like those she really saw me engineering as I peppered her with my youthful dreams and goals.

My dream-bridges are built in places where spans of water are small and few. You couldn't walk across the smallest bubbling brook on my bridges but, on it, people will cross into anywhere their hearts lead them.

I'm working on bridges where people will learn to express themselves through writing; where people of all ages will bring out what glows within.

I'll always see writing and helping others to find their writing voices as the bridge my mother allowed me to build.

It's a mighty bridge.

My bridge already has delivered me across the continent and an entire ocean to work with several generations of people. My bridge has helped young people in Florida realize and express the wonders of fall seasons in Wisconsin.

My bridge has often carried me back to "the land," allowing me to realize its relaxing and comforting value.

Mine is a bridge where I hope many others will be able to cross while opening them to the wonderful world of writing.

Many along the rural routes have found bridges like mine – real and imagined – to cross between the lights of the "other" world and the down-to-earth rural heritage that means so much to us.

I still hope to someday build a real bridge to remind me of the importance of finding our way across the two-way bridge. If I do manage to build such a structure, it won't be anywhere near the one I'd promised to build for Mom. Such a structure also could remind others that a small woman let her little boy's mind wander often enough so he'd believe he really could build the biggest of all bridges.

When my bridge is completed, I'll know Mom is smiling at her son, who built the biggest darned bridge she ever could have imagined.

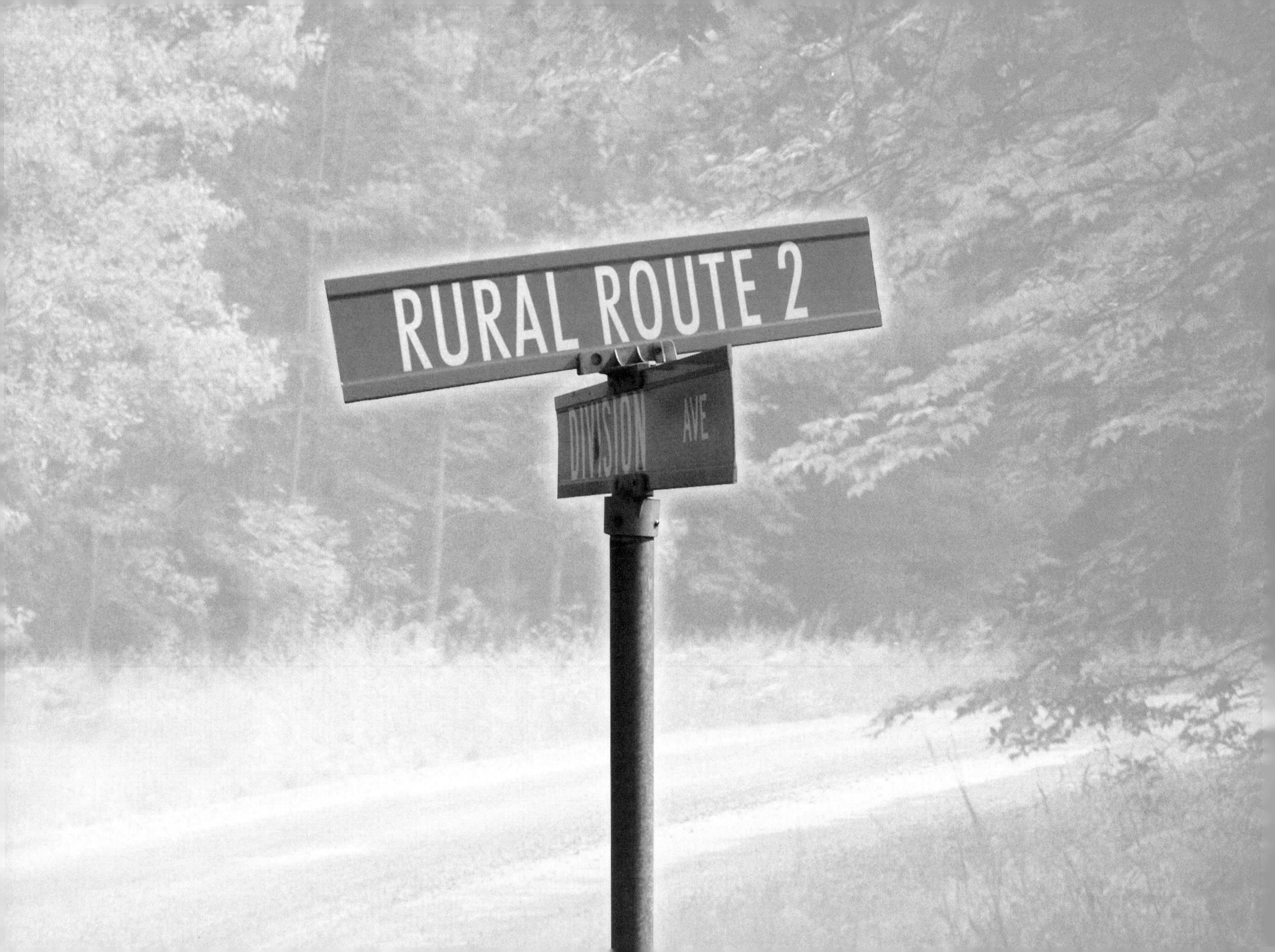
RURAL ROUTE 2
DIVISION AVE

People Along the Route

Knowing Great People

Working in the newspaper business can put a person in contact with plenty of famous people.

My work has indeed done that. I've spoken with governors, future presidents, vice presidents, cabinet secretaries, generals, university presidents, Olympians, actresses, authors and plenty of others who could make me a king of name-dropping.

Life's been good to me in those terms. Who, after all, wouldn't be happy having met people of such fame and influence? It's probably one of the attractions for young people who are considering a journalism career.

I'm glad I've had such a chance, but not because I see it as having elevated my place in the world. Rather, because it made me realize who the world's important people are and where they can be found.

I've found that the people along rural routes truly are the important people of this world.

Evidence of that came early in my life. I watched neighbors gather and travel from farm to farm to help each other cut firewood for the winter. It wasn't as spectacular as stories of neighborhood threshing crews from an earlier era, but it gave me a glimpse of what those down-to-earth people were about.

They worked together and they worked with purpose. The crew showed no particular enjoyment toward their work, but it was clear that no neighbor wanted to fall behind and let his neighbors down. Breaks were taken only for lunch or to light the cigarettes that each man held in his mouth as they worked.

"Nothing is more important than a man's word," my father told me in later years. I'm pretty sure he learned that idea while working with those neighbors. If they said they'd help, they'd be there. If they said they'd work, they'd work.

Today there may no longer be that same kind of neighborhood cooperation. Technology took away much of that need. But many thousands of rural people still are close enough to their past to know values passed down through rural generations.

Those who know such values can see through the glitter of phoniness in politicians, lawyers, salesmen and the like. They're quick with a "hello" and a smile but somewhat cautious in allowing others to know them deeply. Most of them avoid the shine of the spotlight and snicker with each other about self-promoters.

What you see is what you get with great rural people.

The great rural people have done physical labor that late in life hunches them over and makes them limp. "Work" means "work;" there's very little sitting involved. Their work is strenuous; it's never-ending. There is no Occupational Safety and Health Administration to assure their safety. There are no unions to assure a living wage, health and dental plans or acceptable working conditions.

Forty-hour weeks and overtime aren't discussed; there are no such things. The day's work is done until the day's work is done and then it's repeated the next day.

Time away from work might mean no more than a trip to church on Sunday or evening visits with neighbors or relatives. Vacations for many rural people wait until late in their lives.

Churches and schools are the centers of their communities.

A reporter I know once returned from a school where she'd spoken with a foreign exchange student from Europe.

"It's interesting to talk with somebody like that," she said. "They're so much more sophisticated than the people around here."

If the definition of sophistication means getting around the world to see a variety of people and places, then she was right. But I think sophistication means having a good sense of place in the world, to be able to use life experiences to make good judgments, to treat others as they'd want to be treated and to sort out the good from the bad.

When I've sought answers about living, I've seldom turned toward someone who's spent their life away from the land, no matter how many schools they've attended or how many places they've visited. I turn to those people who have a literal sense of down-to-earth sophistication.

Sure, those of fame with whom I've spoken have been interesting. But I'm willing to trade interviews with a dozen famous people in exchange for an interview with someone on a rural route who's close to the land – one of our great rural people.

Warmth with Rural Secrets

The north wind needled through my clothing as I headed down the road for bit of early-morning exercise. It wasn't anything like I expected; as late as it was in March, it was supposed to be a bit warmer, even for that early morning hour.

It wasn't such a bad thing, I thought. I could have been in a much more challenging situation as I felt the bite of such spring-morning cold.

Marie Veefkind, Henry's wife, with their daughter Mary.

Facing the cold that morning was by choice. It's much worse when a person is coerced into it.

The cold stung some sensitive spots on my teeth as I smiled and thought of stories of people who have been fooled into some very cold situations during their visits to farms – one of the many ways farmers have trained themselves to get rid of salesmen, reporters and other folks who take more time than the farmers have.

I've been impressed with so many of the methods used, and getting the unwelcome visitor to stand on the coldest spot on the farm has always been my favorite.

"Whenever I want to get rid of somebody like you, I take them to stand and talk between a couple of my silos," a farmer once told me.

He revealed his secret by telling me to follow him to the spot so I'd know what he meant. We stood there for only a moment before I realized the silos created a wind-tunnel effect – the wind hammering between the silos with at least three times the speed in areas away from the silos.

It wasn't only the wind that played a role in the farmer's scheme. The silos allowed no sunlight to warm the spot anytime during the day, which doubled the chilling effect. It was a mid-June afternoon, but a few moments of loitering in the farmer's secret spot made my skin feel as though it was exposed to the ice and snow of a mid-January night.

The silos, it almost seemed, could filter the wind's warmth and allow only its chill to seep into anyone standing there.

The farmer smiled as he saw the goose bumps rise on my bare arms, which only moments before had been massaged nicely by the early-summer warmth.

"Nope, guys don't hang around here too long to try selling stuff," he said.

I thought for a moment and remembered a similar spot between the silos on our old farm at Veefkind – and, for that matter, similar spots on several farms I'd visited. I also tried, without success, to remember whether anyone had ever invited me to stand between their silos as I visited with them.

Since my visit with that farmer, others have told me that they, too, had often used the "between the silos" method of literally giving a "cold shoulder" (and several other body parts) to unwelcome guests.

There are, of course, many other methods that farmers have used over the years to get rid of uninvited guests.

One guy told me he just looks out the window if he happens to be in the house – a long visit to the bathroom while the visitor stands outside waiting for the door to be answered usually gives the visitor the hint to leave.

Another conveyed he could see his entire driveway with a quick glance through a couple of his barn's windows.

That farmer got his exercise with a quick jaunt up the inside of his silo to disappear from the visitors' sight.

The most creative method might have been the guy who carefully watched his cows after they'd been turned out to a fresh, green pasture for the first time in the summer. If one of the cows happened to have a bit of a cough or a cold in those first days of pasturing, he'd invite visitors to stand in his barn alley – right behind those cows.

Those who have been fully initiated to life on a dairy farm will understand why the unwelcome visitors would be leaving after a few minutes.

However, I admired the direct approach at one farm I'd visited. There, the farmer had tacked a sign to the frame of his farm's front door.

"If I haven't called you and invited you or haven't called you and made an appointment to see you, please get back into your vehicle and leave – and please don't take any gravel with you."

Remembering unique stories and moments such as those on farms have helped to make my life complete, I thought as I completed my run.

Having the ability to understand why the farmers did what they did in order to avoid some of those unwelcome visits had helped to warm me during the run.

It warmed me to know that my membership in the farming fraternity – though perhaps by now considered an "associate member" – still was valid enough that my rural brothers and sisters have continued to share such secrets with me.

The Rural Chase

Jim and a few of his friends wrap up their morning barn chores sometime around 5:30 each morning, long before many of their city friends – and even some farming friends – are stirring.

The schedule is routine for a special group along the rural routes: Go to bed early, get out of bed early, milk the cows early and be ready to hit the road early.

Coyotes are to blame for such a schedule.

Coyotes are creatures that a generation of television viewers has come to understand only as a scheming scoundrel that likes to chase fast birds in the desert country.

When it comes to the rural routes' coyote population, the creatures have little in common with its television image – although Jim and his friends may certainly describe coyotes as scheming scoundrels. The only connection to the show's desert floor would be wind-swept farm fields covered with a foot of snow. The rocks the television coyote hides behind are replaced by trees, stumps and brush.

The most important reality is that the coyotes, seen on television as pursuers and hunters, in this case are the

Rural Routes & Ruts

pursued and hunted. Jim and his friends are the pursuers and hunters.

The coyote hunters' tools are many, but the focus is on hounds and snowshoes. Most of the hunters own between one and a dozen hounds which, in warmer months, specialize as bear-hunting dogs. In winter, the hounds become tracking machines on the coyotes' trails.

Jim said coyotes truly are cunning creatures that require good hunting skills and plenty of strategy and teamwork during a chase. The hunters sometime spend most of a day tracking a single coyote.

Some of the hunters' days are spent sitting in trucks along snow-covered dirt roads while hounds try to pick up the scent of a warm coyote track.

By daybreak, the hunters have scanned the roadsides where coyotes may have crossed hours earlier. Well-trained dogs can use inbred smelling skills to take even a cold track and follow it across several sections of land, to where the coyote is lurking.

The hunters use the baying of their hounds to follow the chase, and then place themselves in positions where the chase may cross a field, a road, or an opening in the woods.

However, the coyotes don't always get to the openings. That might require one or more of a group's hunters to don snowshoes and, on foot, close in on the chase area. Many coyote hunters have become masters of snowshoes and endurance, sometimes crossing 5 or 6 miles of deep snow during a day.

Snow can't be too fluffy, or the hounds can't run well enough. Snow can't be too hard, or the hounds will cut their paws on the icy surface.

When conditions aren't good, Jim and his friends catch up on winter farm projects. Sometimes, they get to take a mid-day snooze.

The hunters know the joy of what they do doesn't always involve pulling the trigger to harvest a coyote, nor is it in collecting government bounties put on the animals or in being paid for pelts.

The fun, the hunters know, is in the camaraderie they find during the hunt. Theirs is a rural brotherhood understood by few.

The hunters care about each other; they care about their friends' dogs.

The camaraderie is a good example of the good things people see along our rural routes.

Hanging with Johnny Possum and Turtle Head

Johnny Possum and Turtle Head were staying over at Breezy's place. So, you see, at least you know where part of the gang is.

In case you worry about missing something from this Northwoods soap opera, it's important to learn the language you'll hear when some rural group like the Black River Bottom Kennel Boys gets together in a place like the Wintergreen Resort after a long day of hunting bear in the "big woods."

I'll admit to having fallen behind a little in my translation skills when I first heard the bartender chatting in the group's special language with one of the Black River Bottom Boys. But, once the bartender and a friend translated their conversation, I fully understood which members of the crew were staying at a local private campground.

There's plenty of that kind of talk when you visit a rural place like the Wintergreen. These are the places that live up to their billing as "resorts" in the truest sense. They're places that are off the beaten path – not the type that cater to the rich and famous, but the kind of place where you can truly march at your own pace.

Everybody knows everybody in a place like Wintergreen and, if they don't, it won't be long before they learn. These are the places where you might not return for a year or two, but where the bartender will still manage to greet you by your first name.

Places like Wintergreen get all the interesting customers, it seems. Take, for instance, the Black River Bottom Boys. Their wives would say they'd appreciate someone taking the "Boys" somewhere far away, except that some of the wives were along for the hunt.

The Black River crew has people who go by names like Sweet William, Scruffy, Thumper, Quad, and Tarzan. They can almost speak their own language and, if you're lucky, one of them might have a child or two along to help translate their conversations.

There are places like Wintergreen all over the rural routes. Most of these places don't even call themselves "resorts." Still, they're places where a fellow feels welcome to stop for a burger and a few laughs. They're places where everybody's interested in who you are and what you're doing. They're places where you can escape a world that forever seems to be moving faster.

Some might say places like the Wintergreen lack sophistication. That's debatable, I think.

Sure, the language might occasionally turn a little blue, but that's what a quick-witted bartender with a 1-inch piece of lead pipe in hand is good for. The verbiage gets cleaned up in a hurry following a single rap on the bar with a good hunk of pipe.

Neckties might be welcome in some of these places but aren't recommended – especially on Saturday nights.

A little mud or cow manure seems to be good for the ambiance in places like the Wintergreen. One thing about a place like that is that customers don't wait until your back is turned to talk about your need for a change of clothes and a shower. If you are, indeed, a bit too ripe for the atmosphere, they'll let you know right away.

People might say Wintergreen-like places are a little too "rednecked" for some tastes. I suppose some of the customers – at least one or two – might be offended by such a stereotype. But, most would sit on their barstools with pride and say "yep, and if you want to see more redneck life, just get yer behind over to Breezy's place and talk with Windy, Turtle Head or Johnny Possum."

Dale's Heroic Lesson

Dale is a pretty easy-going fellow, in my opinion. I've always found that it takes more than a little more prodding to get him riled.

He's a guy who could have a right to wear a frown a lot, to be bitter about an accident a few years back that took the use of his legs and left him with little use of his arms. Dale has had a smile and a wisecrack aimed at me just about every time I've seen him drive his wheelchair into his eatery and tavern along Wisconsin's rural routes.

I've always respected Dale for not letting too many things bother him, for what my opinion counts. He's had enough challenges that taught him to keep things in perspective, I've always assumed.

But a little coolness could be seen in Dale's eyes as he recounted a poaching incident. Some cowards with a spotlight and rifle knocked down the whitetail buck deer Dale had spent a month trying to outsmart, while bow hunting from his wheelchair.

It wasn't just the loss of the deer that bothered him. Even more serious was that the cowards had been shooting toward Dale's ground stand, presenting a dangerous situation.

As it turned out, Dale had better luck at outsmarting the poachers than he'd ever had in outsmarting any of the animals he'd hunted. Dale had the foresight to carry a cellular telephone on his hunt, making it easy for him and his buddy to call a neighbor who's a deputy sheriff. The poachers were apprehended within a few hours.

I was amazed at the details about the poachers that Dale shared with me. I've hunted for many years and never once had thought about doing what those poachers were doing. If the energy the cowards had spent in planning their poaching expedition had been put toward "fair chase" planning, I think they could have had some sportsmanlike hunting success.

Dale's description of their methods helped me figure out what I'd seen as people flashed a light in a ditch a few nights earlier near my own woodlot. Theirs was a signal that the search for their ill-gained deer was over and that the people sitting in a darkened vehicle around the corner of the section should come to pick them up.

At first, I felt naïve about not knowing how those clowns operate at night. Then, however, I had a good feeling about never having stooped to such stupidity and pathetic ethics in order to harvest game.

Later, I even saw some humor in it all. There actually are meatballs who think they're operating under the cloak of darkness, when their million-candlelight spotlights are pinpointing their location to the world. How smart does someone have to be to know that a light is the last thing you want to have in your hand if you're trying to hide in the darkness?

People are concerned that I use words like "coward," "idiot," "doofus," "meatballs" and the like to describe outlawing poachers. It won't bother the poachers, I'm sure, because I really doubt that people like that have the intelligence to be reading a book.

Dale's been a hero for many reasons, in my opinion. By finding a way to corner a few poachers, I'm elevating his hero status a little higher. His actions reminded me that we along the rural routes like the notion of doing things the way they're supposed to be done – and that there's no glory or sport in poaching. Decent people along the rural routes shake their heads in disgust when some doofus tries to impress them with a story of a big buck that couldn't escape a blinding spotlight and a .22 caliber rifle.

Dale might not be able to leap out of his seat when something like this bothers him. But he did a fine job standing up for what's right.

We should all hope to have half of his courage.

A Sad Time for Funeral Foods

I ate a cold cut turkey sandwich the other day, and I didn't enjoy it a bit. Neither did I enjoy the cold cut ham sandwich that I used to wash down the turkey sandwich.

Normally, I'd have found some simple pleasure in either of the sandwiches. Unfortunately, both of them were the entrée at a church funeral lunch.

The fact that I was eating the sandwiches at a lunch following the funeral of one of my real heroes was bad enough to make the sandwiches far less enjoyable than they ever might have been.

I'll vouch that there is little more than pain involved with funerals. Sure, there's a sense of closure and the feeling of support from many friends and family when a loved one is lost, but the sense of loss hurts like no other hurt.

I should know the feeling; as I've come of age and started to reach deeply into my middle-age years, I've had plenty of experience with funerals and the mourning process.

There's loss. There's emptiness. There's uncertainty. There are waves of tears that appear from nowhere as a good memory pops into mind.

Then, to top it off, I stand in the post-funeral lunch buffet line and see the cold cuts.

Having been raised in rural congregations, cold cuts are something that I'd hoped never to see served at a funeral lunch.

Rural church cookbooks include the specialties that deserve to be served at a funeral lunch – the prime dish known around most of rural Wisconsin simply as "funeral casserole." I'm not sure what differences there are between funeral casserole and any other conventional casserole containing ground beef, noodles and maybe some beans. I'm only sure that, when served after the energy-sapping event of a funeral, the funeral casserole offers a level of inner warmth and comfort.

As I think of it, some dictionaries might want to have a picture of a funeral casserole to define "comfort food." Funeral casserole is the original comfort food.

No funeral is complete without several other forms of casseroles to complement the funeral casserole. Usually, they include a combination of beans – the three-bean mixes or the green bean casserole complete with fake fried onion rings crumbled on the top.

Funeral food tells much about where food fits in rural traditions. Historically, the rural route is a waste not-want not world, resulting in wonderful "dump casseroles" and "dump cakes."

The bars are important, too. Having a good selection of homemade bars on a funeral lunch table can have mourners momentarily forget their loss and concentrate on which bar to eat. The best of the bars can even create light debates over who called dibs on a certain bar.

I was at one recent funeral where the debate over a bar became so spirited that a man split the small bar into quarters so that he could share it with three other people who lusted after the bar.

Worries about whether a good funeral casserole will be served or debating who gets a nice-looking bar probably don't seem like appropriate parts of the mourning process. But, I'll argue that those sorts of things are exactly what mourners need at that moment – the relief of having their minds momentarily removed from the depth of loss.

Of course, the loss doesn't really disappear. The pain is still there, for sure. But a top-notch funeral lunch helps at least for a few minutes.

The cold cuts at the recent funeral weren't the worst it could be when I consider that a good part of American society is far removed from the difference over whether funeral casseroles or cold cut sandwiches are served at a funeral lunch. In many parts of the country, I understand, there is no such thing as a lunch following a funeral. Increasing numbers of folks these days even disdain any sort of church funerals.

Still, the cold cuts signal to me the beginning of the end of something that's meaningful to rural routes. People pull together when there is a loss. For many years, pulling together has included having some of the best cooking and baking going on to help ease a neighbor's loss.

It's just a bit of difference in the way society is working, I'd say. The basis of a good, traditional rural church funeral dinner came from ladies who didn't work outside their homes. I won't pass judgment on that sort of thing; I'll just say that I'll miss having funeral casseroles.

I made note of the good funeral casserole served after the funeral of the husband of a workmate. Their church is 10 miles from the nearest town, and it was apparent from the lunch that people along that rural route held many of the traditions I'd known in my youth.

"A priest told me once that people like to come here for funerals because of the lunch," my workmate friend said, her cried-out eyes smiling for one of the few times that week.

There will be a time, I suppose, when even that church has funerals without funeral casserole.

Somehow, I'll have to come up with a way to find warmth in cold cuts.

The Country Doctor

He spoke with a certain softness in his voice as he told me about the pet goose he'd owned as a child. And, even in his advancing years, he towered over me as he showed me the picture of his beloved old Marquette University band.

Those are some of the everlasting memories I have of Dr. A.P. Hable, the man who brought me into this world.

As is the case for most small-town rural doctors, we knew him best only as "Doc Hable" or "Doc." However we knew him, much about the rural route will continue to rekindle memories for most who had contact with him or others like him.

Most of my memories of Doc were built in the eyes of a little boy, sick and scared, going to the doctor with a sore throat.

"Can he take penicillin?" Doc would ask my mother.

I was sure he knew Mom's answer would be "yes," but that he had to ask it just to make sure. A slight prick in the arm, and I'd be ready for action within a few hours.

Some of the visits to Doc were for more serious matters. There was an Easter Sunday when my cousin and I were pecking at each other with our BB guns. A BB hit my right eye, causing me pain throughout the night. The seriousness of the situation sunk in the next morning as Doc examined the eye.

Usually cool and collected, Doc's soft baritone voice had a soothing effect. But when he looked at my eye that morning, he jerked the light-reflecting exam tool from his head and threw it across the room.

"Those goddamn BB guns should be outlawed!" he boomed as the reflector cracked against the far wall.

His reaction told all in his office that something bad had happened. Memories of the two-week hospital stay that followed, and the years that eye specialists gave to save the sight in that eye, pale in comparison to the one moment I ever saw Doc lose his cool.

In quieter moments at Doc's office, people who waited to see him probably found themselves staring at the ancient-looking radio in his outer office and wondering whether it actually worked. People might remember having to go to a room behind his exam area to have a limb x-rayed. Or they might remember how he'd seem to appear from nowhere in the middle of a high school football game to examine an injured player.

Doc Hable was as much a part of my life as anybody while I was growing up. There's little question that country doctors like him were placed on earth for the sake of accident-prone country youngsters.

Doc's service to his community didn't end on his office steps. If the reversible sign on his exam-room door said "The Doctor is Out" when patients entered his office, it probably meant Doc was over at the barber shop, passing along his good cheer and fishing stories. Or, he might have been over at the high school, administering some quick athletic physicals.

Whatever he was doing, it was certain that he was doing it with his firm hand, his soothing voice and his caring heart.

I'd lost track of Doc as years passed. Then, just before he closed his office forever, I took a newspaper assignment to write an account of a dying breed: the people who worked as small-town, private-practice general practitioners.

Doc Hable was perfect for the story.

While interviewing Doc, he shared with me some of the insights of being such a small-town doctor; about the push-and-shove world that medicine was becoming. He told me some things about medicine that I never imagined could cross his lips – stories of greed and selfishness.

Doc was in failing health by the time of the interview, and he bluntly said so. Still, the little boy in me made me believe my personal country doctor was immortal. He needed to be immortal, because there were too many country people who needed him.

Our paths went different directions for about a year after that interview. Then he suddenly appeared next to my desk. He offered me the chance to work with him on a collection of his memories of the many years he'd spent practicing rural medicine – including some that had little to do with medicine but more with his rural life. It was a chance I found impossible to resist.

We spent a good number of hours together with a tape recorder after that, putting together ideas for the collection.

Doc told me plenty of stories during those visits, like the one where a farm chicken hatched a goose egg when Doc was a boy. The goose grew and became a pet, much like a dog, he said. When it came time to kill the goose for a family dinner, Doc protested to his father. Doc's father told him he'd better become a doctor or something, because he'd never make it as a farmer.

Thanks to a goose, Doc eventually delivered me so that I could someday tell his story.

Another of those stories was his eerie recollection of a pack of wolves working through the night to devour a deer, while Doc and his deer hunting buddies listened from the safety of their hunting camp.

Doc shared stories about the antics of his rural friends. He confided to me the exact location of his favorite fishing hole along a 25-mile stretch of a west-central Wisconsin river.

As it turned out, Doc was using his many stories about rural living to cover his concerns about newfangled ways of practicing assembly-line medicine.

We never found the time to get together often enough. Doc's immortality ran out before he could tell me about what I knew was the best to come.

It's a harsh feeling of reality, knowing that Doc and so many others like him are no longer with us on the rural routes.

Since he left us, I've always thought about Doc when I've had a sore throat. But I've also always had the lonely feeling of being in Doc's waiting room, the sign on his exam-room door saying "The Doctor is Out." And the harshness has increased each time I've realized the sign will never again be turned around to say "The Doctor is In."

Harry Puts Up the 'Closed' Sign

There was a simple "closed" sign on the barbershop door.

That might not seem like a big deal to many people, particularly in this age of big malls that have plenty of

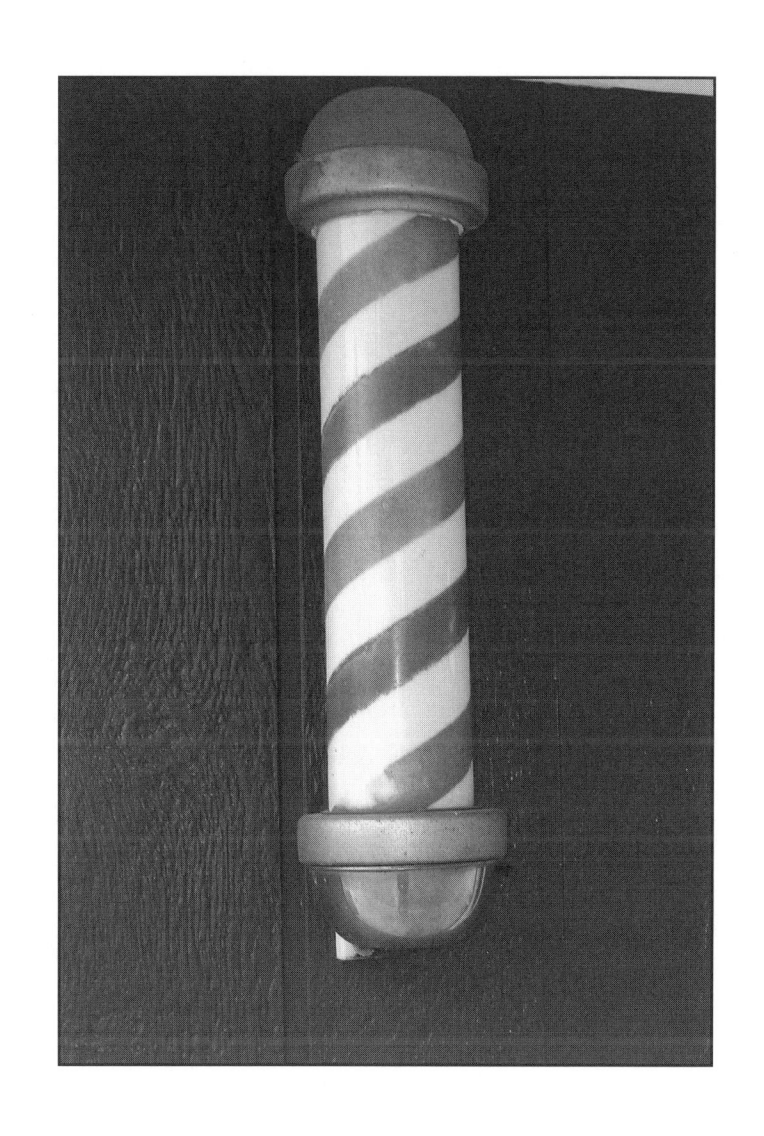

Roaming the Roads of Rural Life

factory-like beauty salons that are more than willing to take a guy's 15 bucks for a trim.

But, it's a big deal around these parts, because there are plenty of guys who have never been to one of those fancy joints and who never want to visit one of them.

In days after the closed sign appeared, my dad and my nephew called me on consecutive days to see if Harry – the barber – had opened his door for business again. Dad called because he was getting up there in years and didn't want to drive the 10 miles into town if the barbershop wasn't open.

Harry was having some health problems, and people talked across cups of coffee about whether he would be back in business. The concerns were more about Harry's health than whether their hair could be trimmed that week. But, there was an undertone of worry about whether the rural community could be without its barber.

There were no fancy announcements or anything, but Harry answered questions in a simple manner for all those who ever cast a shadow upon his shop's door. A thank-you note in the community's weekly newspaper made the closing official:

"I am retiring from barbering. Thank you for being my customers for 46 years. God bless you all. – Harry Francis. The Barber."

Closing.

That's a pretty strong word when you're talking about a place where so many of us received our first haircuts; a place where we heard our grandfathers answer questions about looking for the big muskies like the one hanging on the shop's wall.

Closing is a strong word about the place where you could count on guys like Doc Hable to stop a couple of times a day to rattle off a few words of wisdom.

No disrespect to the "beauty salons" around town; I've had my hair cut in those places plenty of times. But, there was something uniquely male about barbershops like Harry's. I can't remember too many "salons" with a magazine selection topped by Field and Stream and Outdoor Life. I'd bet the chances are 100-to-1 that you'll find a newspaper like The Country Today in a barbershop long before you'd find a magazine touting the latest hair styles.

Other businesses also would never have a code of honor like a barbershop, where guys who aren't particularly busy would be happy to let a busier fella jump into the chair first.

Without the rural barbershops, there won't be anymore haircuts costing much less than $10; no more places where the phrase "a trim and a shave for 2 bits" was coined. There won't be a place where an appointment consists of a guy sticking his head in to ask "how many ahead" and have the barber answer "you have time to stop at the feed mill and the hardware store."

There isn't a place where a dad can take his son for a first haircut among the men, or where a boy can beam with pride when he graduates out of the barber's lift-seat and can sit on the chair like the grown-ups do.

I guess the local barbershop is another of those things I'll start having to accept as only part of a rural community's history – just like the canning factories, the five-and-dime store and full-service filling stations.

Time rolls on. But, with the closing of any of those historic places goes a little piece of life from each of us on the rural route.

Getting a Gizzard Check

"Hey Cooter, how's your gizzard?"

For many years, that greeting was music to my ears. It meant that my old neighbor and friend was nearby.

I never could totally figure out what made him such a friend or what made him so interesting to me. In another time or another place, he might have been just another guy named Lester living in the first place up the road from our farm.

He was more than "Lester." He was "LESTER."

The relationship I shared with Lester started when I broke into his house. I didn't know I was breaking in at the time, and Lester and his wonderful wife, Myrtle, didn't seem to mind.

Lester and Myrtle simply watched, somewhat stunned, as their 5-year-old neighbor boy roamed past them while they ate lunch at their kitchen table. They sat silently as I strode up to their refrigerator, opened its door and pulled out a couple of sticks of celery.

They told me years later they were equally as mesmerized by watching me close the refrigerator door and walk out of the house, munching on a stick of celery without having said a word.

It was the one time in his life when Lester didn't see me and give me his "Hey Cooter, how's your gizzard?" greeting.

A few days later, in the presence of my parents, Lester and Myrtle told me there would always be celery for me in their refrigerator, and they'd be happy to see me come in and take some whenever I felt the urge. I took them up on their offer and, in a Dennis the Menace-like fashion, I let myself into their house many times after their offer – always receiving that "Hey Cooter, how's your gizzard?" greeting from Lester whenever he happened to be home during my celery run.

I'm not sure why Lester picked "Cooter" as a nickname for his red-headed cowlick-haired neighbor. I never asked him for fear that he meant I reminded him of some sort of little critter, like a "cootie." More likely, I've believed – hoped – it was short for "Scooter," a nickname many use for little boys named "Scott."

Most in the neighborhood knew after a long day of work and a tavern stop for a boilermaker (a shot of booze followed by a glass of beer), Lester may not have known exactly whether he was saying "Scott" or "Cooter" – or, for that matter, whether he was saying "Harold" or "Chester."

Lester was a tinkerer. When not at work as a truck driver or in a factory, Lester was working the five acres around his home as though it was a 1,000-acre farm. Naturally, working that sort of acreage with a small tractor and other aging, small-acreage equipment, Lester had his hands full with the work that needed to be done. He would tear apart his aging little tractors and put them back together. Sometimes the repairs worked, sometimes they didn't.

Lester was fairly handy with a welder. In the vernacular of a machine shop, he could "lay a pretty good bead."

He planted trees that he knew would become valuable as years passed. When he was up to it during a given spring, he'd plant some vegetables.

His favorite spots seemed to be his basement or garage workshops.

On occasion, I knew a metalworking project would be as good, or better, in Lester's hands as it would in the hands of the local blacksmith. It also was a goodly amount less expensive to accept Lester's offer to do the project for virtually nothing. This was one of the things that impressed me about him.

His understanding of medicine also impressed me, but as much out of sarcasm as it was for his real medical understanding. I knew Lester as one of the few people who, as he aged, personally pulled every one of his own teeth. He used no prescribed painkillers to extract them. The only painkillers he'd need were a couple of pulls from one of the fifths of booze he liked to have at a handy place (a handy place being a pocket, a workbench, the underside of a car seat, the crotch of a tree…).

While I was impressed by the toughness Lester exhibited by pulling his own teeth, his practice had its critics. One of my brothers, suspecting that Lester's dental hygiene may not have been sparkling, suggested that pulling a tooth from Lester's gums was "like pulling a stick from the swamp."

Whatever sounds were made when Lester pulled those teeth, and however unimpressed anyone might have been with that feat, anyone would have been impressed with the way Lester could devour steaks, chewing the meat with his hardened gums much as a person with the strongest teeth could. I've often considered how lucky he must have been after eating a steak: he never was left with the discomfort of having a piece of meat stuck between his teeth.

I suspect it was the partially chewed food landing in Lester's intestinal tract that led to much of Lester's abdominal pain in his later years. It was that same abdominal pain that, upon his return from a nearby clinic, led Lester to utter one of the most profound things that I've ever heard.

"That damned doctor's a fool," Lester said. "I sat there waiting for him for an hour. When he finally got in by me, he asked me what the problem seemed to be. I said, 'How to hell do I know? You're supposed to be the doctor!'"

Much about Lester's lifestyle may not have been exemplary. He smoked unfiltered Camel cigarettes until he died in his late 80s; he would have been happy with an entire diet of fried eggs and side-pork. Despite his happiness in eating fatty fried foods, much of Lester's skeleton seemed to nearly stick through the skin of his slight structure.

His skin-and-bones appearance may have been from a metabolism driven wild by his chain smoking, combined with gallons of coffee.

Lester shared plenty of his coffee with me in his later years, long after Myrtle's death. The coffee was of questionable flavor, its consistency similar to the silt on the bottom of the nearby Yellow River. It took a while for me to learn that the coffee's texture and hair-raising strength indeed came from Lester's method of conserving coffee and coffee filters.

Instead of removing the filter and used coffee at the completion of every pot, Lester would simply throw another tablespoon of fresh coffee into the machine's basket, reusing the grounds and filters three or four times.

The flavor of the coffee didn't matter during my visits to his kitchen. I drank plenty of it during those times when, as an adult, I walked into his house without having knocked. Without saying anything besides "hi" to Lester, I'd walk to his kitchen cupboard and pour two cups of coffee. I'd carry them to the table where Lester sat – his many bad habits by then having taken a serious toll on his health – and sit with him for an hour or two of hunkered-down rural conversation.

Lester started each of those conversations in a wonderfully predictable way.

"Hey Cooter, how's your gizzard?"

Alfred was a Fair Man

Old Alfred huffed and puffed more than a little as he pushed a wheelbarrow through one of the horse barns at the county fairgrounds.

It was difficult for him to straighten his back. He struggled to keep the wheelbarrow's two iron rear stands from gaining even a quick touch of the straw scattered on the barn's concrete floor. His long years of farm labor had drained much of his strength, and he always remained somewhat hunched over as a result, even when not negotiating a wheelbarrow through a barn – giving him a somewhat rounded appearance.

Rural Routes & Ruts

Alfred had been cleaning up after some of his family's prized Belgian horses, a chore that he'd repeated thousands of times during his life. It was a chore of love, a chore that helped him remember the days when his strong, still-straight body could move shovels and forks in ways that made work get done in a hurry.

Horses had been part of his entire life, and he often talked proudly about them. His pride showed in the way the animals stood and in the way they pulled his show-wagons. It showed in the way their manes and tails were perfectly groomed, and in the way their reddish-brown hair gleamed.

A special pride shone in Alfred's eyes on that day, however.

The work was being done in the momentary absence of his many boys, whom he said he was "giving a break." The boys all were well into their adult lives and even had sons and daughters who all shared their fathers' and grandfather's pride in the Belgian horses.

The boys had been doing the chores without so much help from Alfred in recent years and deserved the break he was giving them, Alfred said in his raspy voice.

The wheelbarrow's back legs never touched the floor as Alfred talked. He held its long, wooden handles and occasionally rocked his weight from one leg to the other, balancing the implement's load on its single wheel. Despite the overflowing load being a nasty byproduct of a horse barn, Alfred reminded me that his chore was one that helped him remember the good and simple things in life.

As his boys' return neared, Alfred talked proudly about his offspring and seemed even more excited to speak of his many grandchildren.

There were 16 of his grandchildren exhibiting projects at that county fair. He said he'd really wanted to give his sons a break from the horse barn so the boys could watch the judging of his grandchildren's projects. After all, he said, a parent should have the same opportunity to see his child "show off" just as many years earlier he'd watched his sons.

He also said he was happy about the number of his grandchildren exhibiting fair projects. He was a firm believer that children who did well with fair exhibits generally didn't turn out to be bad apples.

He told of how a judge he'd known had taken a keen interest in children who exhibit projects at county fairs.

The judge had once told Alfred that he couldn't remember a single successful youth fair exhibitor ever appearing in one of his courtrooms. Alfred surmised that, if the judge wasn't exaggerating, it must have been a good thing if so many of his grandchildren were participants in the fair.

Alfred said the judge must have known something about youth. In that case, Alfred said it was worth every bit of the extra work that he was doing so his boys could be off supporting his grandchildren's work in exhibiting.

The evening was getting on as Alfred told me about more of the experiences his family had while exhibiting at that county fair. But he kept getting back to the notion of how having 16 grandchildren exhibiting projects at the same county fair must have been some sort of a record.

Alfred must have been pretty proud about that, and he was probably pretty proud about the prizes his grandchildren hauled home from that fair.

He also was proud to have been able to give his boys a break from the Belgians, even though he'd reached a point in life when just a couple of turns around a dance floor could quickly tucker him out. But in Alfred's case, that would be another story for another time.

The fatigue that the work had brought on him didn't stop him from putting in a few good words about his children and grandchildren, a habit he and many of his long-time rural neighbors had gained.

He could have stopped talking about those children, and it surely would have conserved some of his energy.

He could have remembered to set the wheelbarrow down as he spoke.

Neither mattered as he told his history.

Alfred is gone and his grandchildren have grown to be adults. His boys take turns giving breaks to their children so Alfred's great-grandchildren can have support with their fair exhibits.

In a special way, the rear legs of Alfred's wheelbarrow still aren't touching the straw on that barn's floor.

Playing Through Pain

Green Bay Packers legend has it that, after one of his players was diagnosed with a broken leg-bone, Coach Vince Lombardi said, "That's not a weight-bearing bone, get out there and play!"

Playing with pain is an idea that has given hero status to plenty of athletes. Sports fans marvel whenever an athlete fights through pain to compete at a high level.

But little is ever said about those who go about their daily business and work through pain.

Pain happens, and it happens on a regular basis in the rural world.

Farms are places where worker's compensation usually doesn't happen. It's a place where cows must be milked, where cattle must be fed. Chores must be done and, when help is short, the person in charge must do them, no matter how sick or hobbled that person is.

Strange as it may be, rural people are apt to work through injuries or illnesses even when help is available.

I've often thought about my father's hands in his later years, when you could see the results of jammed and broken fingers, the ends of a couple of his digits turned at 45-degree angles away from the rest.

I've recalled his long struggles with a hernia. He said for years that he should have it repaired.

"When it pops out, I just take a finger and push it back in," he'd say, until the day he tried to pick up the tongue of our John Deere 14T baler.

His attempt at picking up the baler hitch ripped his hernia open to the point where only a skilled surgeon could "push it back in." His pain finally made him relent and go to a hospital. There, a doctor told Dad that surgery would have to be performed on the hernia.

Dad insisted on going home later that afternoon to do chores and give instructions to his sons — maybe to return for the surgery the next day. The doctor calmly made Dad realize how the surgery was going to be done within minutes — not within the next couple of days.

I've remembered many farming neighbors who, by mid-life, could barely walk. Those farmers' knees were decimated by millions of turns at squatting beside dairy cows.

At least a dozen farmers I know are missing a foot, a leg, fingers, part of a hand or part of an arm. Those farmers put their limbs in places not meant for limbs and have paid a big price for the rest of their lives. But once healed, every one of them continued to work on their farms.

One day a few years ago, one of my friends called to tell me how something he'd seen earlier that day assured him that my son, Jamie, would have a very successful year in high school wrestling. The friend had seen the concrete crew on which Jamie was working as the crew stopped for gas at a nearby town's convenience store. The top of one of Jamie's hands had been cut fairly seriously that morning and then patched the way real working stiffs would patch such a cut.

"Any guy who cuts his hand that badly, patches it with a handkerchief and duct tape and then goes back to work has to have something going for him," the friend said.

I'm one to join the legions of people who respect athletes who overcome some pain to play a game.

But, I'm one who gets downright reverent toward those rural people who fight through real physical challenges and often do what needs to be done. There's no fanfare for those people — just the satisfaction of knowing they did another day of honest labor.

Rural Routes & Ruts

Falling and Rising with a November Full Moon

The old farmer barely noticed the corn leaf resting on his forehead. A combination of the growing numbness in his body and the many thoughts racing through his mind seemed to be much more important than such a minute detail.

It was getting on 6 p.m. on that cool November evening, and he realized as he lay among the mud and corn stubble in one of his fields that it would likely be many hours before he was found. He'd already resigned himself to the fact that he wasn't going anywhere in the meantime – each time he moved, the pain in his hip was enough to make tears stream down his weathered cheeks.

During the previous half-hour – he wasn't sure how long, actually, because time was becoming less important to him as each moment passed – he'd considered what people would say about his situation. There would be sorrow, he was sure, but there would be friends and neighbors shaking their heads in disbelief that he'd chosen that time of day for a walk in a freshly-picked corn field.

The moon had drawn him there in the first place, the same moon that still shone brightly over the barn and two silos that once housed his small herd of Holsteins.

Before this "situation" occurred, he'd been slowly strolling along, enjoying the large orange ball of the November full moon as it rose between his silos. During the many years that had passed since his younger days – when he'd last taken time to stop and see the moon – he had thought about what it might look like.

Much was the same as when, as a child, he'd seen the moon rise from that vantage point, he thought. His youthful energy had been slowed when he saw it back then, and he was drawn to sit in corn stubble. He had watched the splendor from nearly the same spot where now the last of his energy was draining from his body.

As time had passed on this night, his senses had been alerted to many of the same things he'd felt, seen, heard and smelled during his initial visit to that spot.

The air at that time of the day had the same bite as it did then, putting the chill of death into the field's muddy soil.

The soil still had the same smell, too: the manure spread there last winter mixed with the local silt loam that he always felt had its own special odor. It wasn't the same as it was in the spring, when the plow breaking the sod brought forth the soil smell, which for many years had signaled "new growth." The soil at the end of the growing season instead had a "flat" odor he'd always thought was its way of communicating its need for a long winter's nap.

As near to the ground as he was, there was no need for the breeze to carry the corn stalks' aroma into his nostrils; it was pleasantly overwhelming. It was that unique odor that had sealed his decision to walk into the field, its allure making him ignore the deep ruts left by the harvesting equipment. As he saw the moon appearing over the horizon, the stalks' scent had reminded him of the last time he'd watched the spectacle from this field.

There was no need for him to remove his yellow chore gloves to know the feel of the cool, damp soil. And he wouldn't need to take more steps to feel the extra heft his boots had picked up while walking through a mixture made by corn waste and the earth's mud.

He had listened as the sharp wind snapped through the stubble, the gusts occasionally swirling dried leaves across the field. The old corn stalks rustled, but it was a different sort of rustle than the one he'd so often heard in green, standing fields of corn. In November, the corn leaves made a sound more like someone crunching cellophane than like the sounds made by his maples and oaks during the summer.

As he silently continued to watch the moon shrink as it rose higher over the silos, he started to wonder whether his work had been worthwhile.

He'd heard the loud crack of his hip as he stumbled into the rut left by the tractor, and the initial pain had been immense. As the initial shock had subsided, he remembered the many physical pains he'd had during the past 20 years. More than 65 years of hard labor on his family's farm had taken physical tolls on virtually every joint in his body. His right knee would barely bend any longer, the result of the many thousand deep-knee bends he'd done to milk his farm's Holsteins. His pain had been constant in his knees, hips, back, hands and shoulders.

A gust of wind jarred the corn leaf resting against his forehead. Then, as though taking on a life of its own, it swirled high above him and became silhouetted against the moon's white brightness.

That's when he knew those many years of work had paid him handsomely. His pay wasn't in dollars, but in what country nights like this have to offer. He smiled as he considered the money he'd have earned had he received a dollar for every time his farm and the rural countryside had made him happy over the years.

The sights, the smells, the sounds, the feel: to him, his rural home had it all. Then, he looked down at his aged legs and thought how similar they looked to the corn stalks snapped over by the picker. It wouldn't be long, he knew, before his crumpled being and the crumpled cornstalks would be rejoined with his beloved soil.

He returned his eyes to the corn leaf. It continued to float toward the white orb of the moon, which by then was directly above the barn.

And his pain was eased.

A Trophy Message

The message on her refrigerator door was as universal as the snow covering her farmyard. It also was as unique as each snowflake falling to become part of the white blanket.

"Grandma, I got a six-point buck. Jeremy."

It was nearly Christmas, and the message had been written a few days before Thanksgiving, nearly a month earlier.

It's not that Jeremy's grandma hadn't gotten around to wiping the erasable marker that formed the words on the small message board. And it certainly wasn't that she had forgotten to erase it.

Grandma stopped anyone who got within sight of the refrigerator, to ensure the visitor's undivided attention was drawn to the message. She beamed with pride as each person acknowledged the accomplishment.

"Isn't it nice that Jeremy got a buck? He always makes sure to let me know when he does something important."

Some rural people take for granted the special messages like the one Jeremy wrote to his grandma. They may be scoffed at by city people. But for my friend, that message is what makes her heart beat; it provides the fuel for warming the blood flowing within her. It's her life.

My friend had been widowed for a little more than a year at the time. Visits by her children and grandchildren had been her salvation. Her large farm house could become lonely, especially around holidays such as Thanksgiving and Christmas.

Pride runs deep across the rural world, and it runs in many directions in most families. Grandparents beam with pride over their grandchildren's accomplishments, while grandchildren take pride in seeing affirmation in their grandparents' eyes.

I'm pretty sure the pride exchanged through hunting accomplishments is quite an ancient thing. It's easy to imagine the joy older people had when the younger people in their family were successful in their hunt.

In those earlier days, the issue likely reached more deeply than simple pride. Theirs was sincere joy, since their very lives depended on the success.

These days, few people who live along America's rural routes sustain themselves with the harvest of the hunt. For most, that hunted bounty is only a treat to go with food produced on farms.

Jeremy's family truly enjoys the taste of the hunted harvest. And his family, like so many others in his part of the rural world, would still easily survive without the wild bounty.

But it's not the need for food that drives members of families like Jeremy's to trouble themselves with spending many hours in the woods.

A much deeper, underlying factor is involved. A natural hunter lies in us all, which ties us to hundreds and even thousands of years ago when successful hunts really did mean the difference between living and dying; those times when hunters were revered with near-religious zeal. From that history wells the pride that prompts young men like Jeremy to carry on the tradition of hunting.

It's a rite of passage.

Jeremy spent the required time preparing and finding the right stand; he spent the required time sitting and waiting. He was patient and still.

Jeremy shot straight and sure.

In the end, Jeremy proved that, if necessary, he would have what it takes to harvest the meat protein for his family – just as ancestors many generations past did for their families.

Older hunters understand the importance of Jeremy's accomplishment, though the deer isn't one that would be a trophy most hunters would want to hang on a wall.

Maybe the antlers from Jeremy's deer won't hang on a wall. It doesn't matter.

Jeremy's trophy was flaunted when he took an erasable marker in-hand and wrote such a simple message on his grandma's message board.

"Grandma, I got a six-point buck. Jeremy."

The pride, affirmation and adoration bubbled from his grandma each time she looked at the note. Jeremy's trophy was on his grandma's refrigerator door and reflected in his grandma's smile.

Rural Routes of the Heart

When Gunner moved to the United States, he made it his home – all of it.

He has smelled newly plowed sod and cut hay drying in the fields. He's seen the changing colors of maple trees in the fall and inhaled the dry air of Death Valley.

Gunner, in his late 60s, left his German homeland 12 years earlier for a job in New York. Then, he spent 10 years walking across the nation's rural routes.

"This is my home, all of it," Gunner said, making a sweeping, 360-degree gesture toward the horizons.

His possessions included the clothes he wore and whatever essentials would fit in the 650-pound box mounted on motorcycles wheels, which he pulls behind him.

Gunner, a master sausage maker, started to think about getting out to see a little of the country after working a couple of years in New York. He sat with me in a rural community's bowling alley and reminded me plenty about what I like about the rural routes.

"One time, it comes in my head. I want to see America, my new homeland," he said.

Roaming the Roads of Rural Life

He saw his new homeland by walking across every state.

Gunner stopped walking only long enough to rest overnight or to find temporary work to sustain his journey. During warmer months, he traveled northern states. He moved south during winter.

The closest thing he had to a traveling companion was a large, wooden crucifix, carved by a man in Germany and given to him before he left for the United States.

"My friend carved it and told me this be good for luck and to not forget your friend," Gunner said through his heavy German accent.

During his stops, Gunner pulled the crucifix from his traveling box and either stood it against something near him or hung it on a nearby tree branch. The box became his bed for the night, a red sleeping bag within keeping him warm.

"I sleep usually under the stars," he said. "For rain, I pull shut the cover."

People along the way offered help, including shelter for the night. Only during the worst weather conditions did he accept shelter beyond that provided by his box. He stayed at a Wisconsin farm one night while tornadoes tore through the countryside.

"It be bad," Gunner said, exhaling smoke from the draw of his Swisher Sweet cigar the day after the storms. "I'm lucky to find that spot."

Gunner enjoyed meeting and learning about new people along the way, but he liked a degree of privacy so he could enjoy the quiet of rural roadsides. He dealt harshly with people who tried to be pushy with him, and told about an encounter with one nosy man.

"He come in where I was and said, 'who owns that box out there?' I answer, 'I do.' The man says 'what's in it?' I says, 'a man's body who asks Gunner twice what's in the box – I shoot him dead for asking twice, and there be plenty of room in there for another man.'"

Only an occasional small smile crossed his tanned, weather-beaten face. He revealed little about his past, other than being born near Munich in Bavaria and that he had virtually no family remaining in Germany.

I was jealous as Gunner told me of the time he'd had for thinking while "between nowhere," the description he used for the most rural of the nation's rural routes. Many ideas popped into his head during the travels, including a book he planned to write when he became too tired to continue his journey.

"I be thinking of a title all the time, driving me nuts," he said.

The title, "Hiking with Jesus," hit him one day as he thought about the meanings behind the crucifix he hauled in his box.

He said the book would have memories about the wonder, beauty and challenges of being on the road for so long. He would tell about smelling the ocean air. The endless sky covering Montana's mountains would be included; as would the historic places where he stood and discussed life with elders of southwestern Native Americans.

There would be descriptions of looking up into California's redwoods, which he described as "more beautiful than any building in this shit world." The book would tell how he temporarily lost his sight from the intense sun while crossing the Mohave Desert.

Gunner told how he breathed in the smell of the land when he came upon a recently plowed field or a new-cut hay field in Wisconsin or Minnesota.

Gunner told of his staple daily diet of dark coffee, peanut butter and bread, followed by a day of eating bread, coffee and peanut butter.

East of the Mississippi, he hunted and fished to supplement his diet. He would scavenge road-kill if he actually saw the vehicle hit the animal.

In his book, Gunner said he'd have tales of the many people he'd met along his rural routes.

And, he said he'd address his quest for truth. He'd address his determination and his belief that, if a person has an idea, they should work on it until the idea becomes reality.

Americans need to appreciate what they have across the countryside, Gunner said. As he saw it, his journey was about just another American living out his dreams.

In following his dreams, he was lucky enough to feel, hear and breathe in all of America.

"That's the enjoyable side," he said. "It's hard work pulling that wagon. But, when you see or smell something, it goes into your heart. That stays with you for your lifetime."

I feel lucky to know what Gunner meant when he said that, and I'm sure others I've known along my own rural routes understand it, too.

It's in our hearts, and it will never leave.

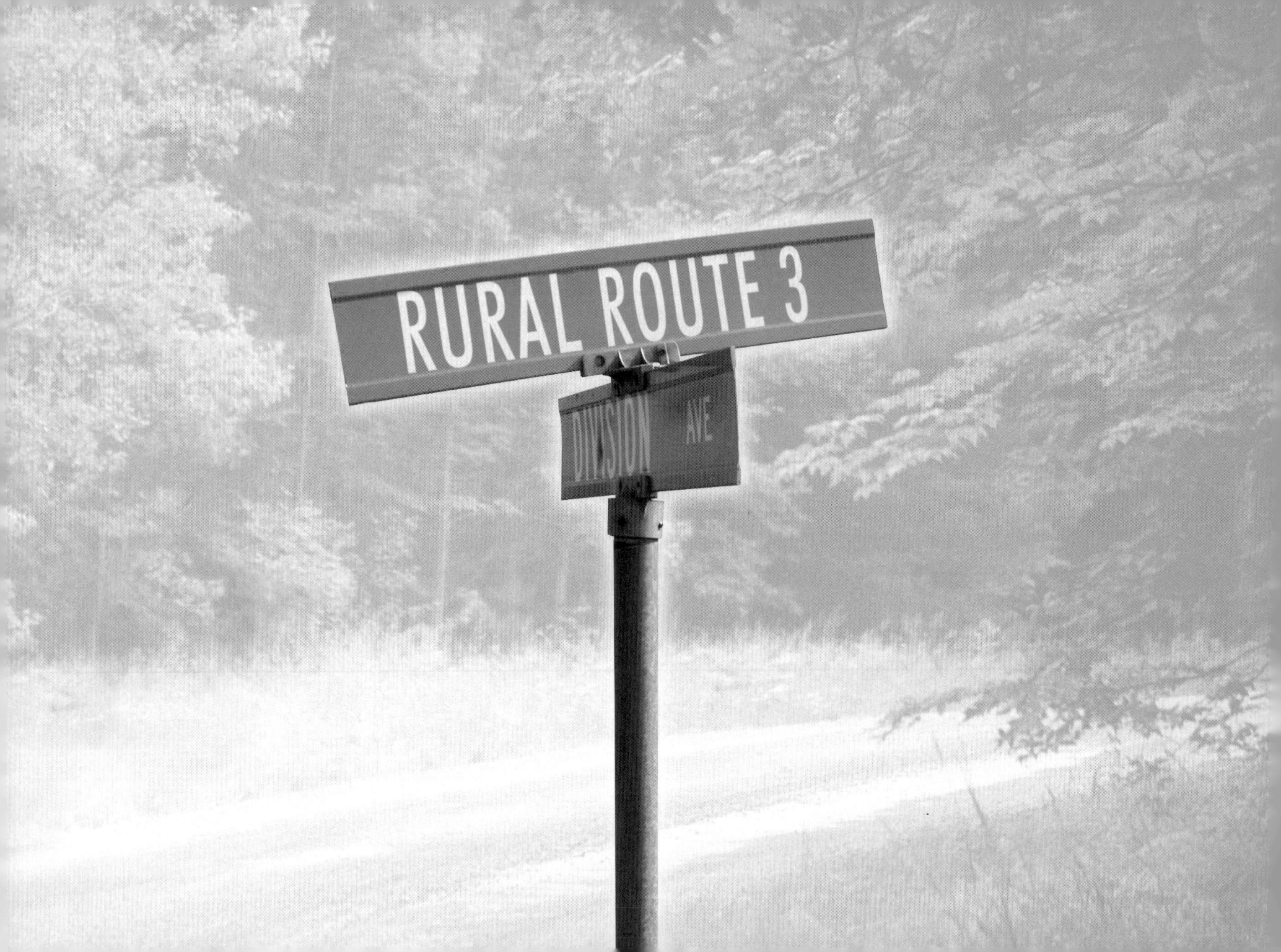
RURAL ROUTE 3
DIVISION AVE

Rural Elements

Facing January from a Barn Door

Steam rolled from the barn's door at a farm I visited on a cold January morning. It was as though the barn was belching out all the energy stored from nearly a full day and night of biology – good and bad – generated by 70 head of Holstein cows.

With the door open and the temperature hovering somewhere around zero, I knew it would be only moments before things near the doorway would be frozen.

It was a reality that would come to pass despite the inability of anyone to even see the process. The dense fog created by the meeting of extreme cold from the outside and the warmth held within that style of barn would hide from sight the frost and ice that would quickly form in the natural refrigeration unit.

I knew the barn's owner learned many years ago the effects of such a process when he opened that door each cold winter morning. He would release the animals from their stanchions to allow the cows to roam the frozen barnyard and then would quickly shut the door to halt the freezing process. After all, fixing a frozen drinking cup in the stall closest to the door is never a good way to finish the morning chores.

It all made me think about January in rural Wisconsin and what each of us might think is the best means of receiving January.

The trouble with the month is that it's such a dark month. Even though the days technically are getting longer, winter's shortage of daylight seems to start wearing on us by about the middle of January. Although a January day can be as bright – with reflections from the snow, sometimes brighter – as any spring or summer afternoon, the length of darkness can start to become overwhelming. With the power of a 16-pound maul driving a steel fencepost into a swamp, it can pound the cold deep into our bones.

Like the frozen soil walked upon by cows in that farm's barnyard, the January cold settles into us with a hardness far greater than anything we'd felt in November or December; the cold creeps and sinks deeply into our being just as the frost drives into the soil.

We know the cold works hard to reach into us. The cold seems ecstatic when it can hit us with a blast such as the one I know the farmer received when he broke that barn door from its icy shackles and flung it open. Or, it can get to us in more stealthy ways, using the wind to reach its stinging tentacles through the smallest of spaces. Warmth can be present and allow us to seek it; cold seeks us.

The farmer standing in the open doorway knows a pinhole-sized draft will do as much damage to his barn's water pipes as would the cold bursting through that doorway. He remembers the feel of hot water running inside his coat's sleeves as he'd so often poured hot water onto newly-frozen water pipes, and the memory of the chilling dampness following that damp warmth makes him do all that he can to keep the cold from finding its prey of steel and water.

The January cold is to be fought off with passion. It's evil. It's the cold of death. It's the cold of knowing no hope.

Still, we somehow manage to find hope, an ability that can be found deep in our rural heritage.

We know the squeaking and clacking sounds made by cows' hooves on the cold-sterilized snow and ice of that barnyard will too soon be replaced by the suction-like sounds of hooves passing through the filthy mud of the same barnyard.

There are some who will submit to the lack of hope harbored by the January cold. But it won't be that farmer in the doorway. He will open the door and face the cold tomorrow, the next day and the next.

Certainly, there will be a day when he no longer will be able to open that door. But we can be at ease knowing it won't be because he was defeated by a few cold January mornings. As with everything about his farm, he will have fought a noble fight. He will have always known the hope he held for warmer days.

Gems from the Country Sky

There was a time, probably not so long ago, when I, like so many others, believed diamonds came from the ground.

As far as I knew, miners dug diamonds out of the depths of the earth after they developed over many thousands of years. Then, the jewelers' artful skills chipped and chiseled to bring individualized glitter to the ancient gems.

Recently, however, I've noticed they don't always come from the earth's bowels. I've seen them fall from the sky.

They fell by the zillions the other day. I saw it happen as I walked along a country road to look at the splendor of a rural Wisconsin winter.

The year's first snow had been late in coming and I was appreciating its freshness – its brightness and clean whiteness finally hiding the dullness of the year's dead and dormant vegetation. The cold winter air pierced my lungs as it already had for many weeks of the winter. With the brightness of the fresh snow, I hadn't even noticed the overcast sky.

Something started to fall from the sky just then. I knew from living so many years of winters that it seemed almost too cold to snow. I thought about how interesting it would be to see what sort of precipitation a razor-sharp cold day such as this could bring.

It was diamonds.

Most people who have experienced a few winters have occasionally seen such diamonds. The cold air apparently works as a diamond cutter's tools, carefully crafting each snowflake as it falls in the freeze-drying conditions.

The diamond flakes aren't the sort that would make a winter outdoorsman blink as the flakes gather in his eyelashes. They aren't even the type of snowflakes that a child would bother to catch on his tongue; the diamond-like flakes would be more likely to steal the wetness from a child's tongue than to add the frozen joy of snow cone-like wetness.

It's surprising that such light flakes even have the mass to reach the ground – that light upper-air breezes don't carry them back into the moisture-deprived clouds that tried to produce genuine snow.

To my delight, the flakes managed to find their way to the fluff-covered surface, their miniscule weight assuring that they'd light gently enough to remain on top of the previous day's snow.

The newly fallen diamonds scattered themselves perfectly across the country fields and yards. Their brilliance was showcased as the afternoon sun started to shine through holes in the clouds, then as the full moon shone across the cloudless winter sky.

With the moon full and nary a cloud in the sky that evening, I trekked out to the same spot where I'd seen the diamonds earlier that day. I stood in awe, looking across the field at the treasure I'd found and momentarily felt like a jewel thief, having heisted those precious gems without paying for them; having received them without deserving them.

I remembered having seen such a display many times before, not knowing for so many years how much such a simple act of nature could be appreciated.

The appreciation I felt was genuine and deep and made me long for someone to be there sharing the wonder with me. Somewhere, I knew, young lovers were doing just that as they strolled along a similar road and saw the brightness of those diamonds; the gems gleaming in their eyes as the lovers gazed at each other for the first time. Somewhere, I knew, there were old lovers who saw the brightness of the diamonds gleaming in their eyes, bringing back the magic of those early years when such glimpses were so special.

What a shame, I momentarily thought, that unlike the diamonds that came from the ground, those country diamonds from the sky wouldn't last forever.

Then I remembered how, like so much of the beauty of the rural countryside, the diamonds would last forever in the soul of anyone like me who'd seen their brilliance glistening in the moonlight.

The diamonds couldn't be picked up and attached to any jewelry that could ever be sold. Those who saw them could only wear them in their memory and their heart.

That's a fair trade, I thought. It's a trade that makes diamonds from the sky the most valuable of all jewels – definitely priceless.

Simple Things in Life Appreciated

I'm convinced winter happens best in the woods.

It was there, while I slapped wet chore gloves together, that the reality of everything winter is about sank deep into my being.

There are signs of winter everywhere by the time December arrives. The signs are in large, beautiful snowflakes falling onto the streets of rural communities on chilly December nights. The signs are in the still small, but ever-growing roadside snowbanks that we see through much of Wisconsin and Minnesota.

Signs of winter are in the crunching sound the snow makes underfoot as you walk to the barn. It's in the freezer-like environment of a silo that has a broken-down silo unloader.

Winter is found in the memories of anyone who has ever hauled manure onto a field on a morning when the temperature drops below zero.

Those signs hang with us like hoarfrost on a bright January morning. But, they pale in comparison to the message nature sends about the presence of winter during visits to a woodlot when the temperature is low and the snow is getting high.

Winter changes everything in the woods. Even the simple task of walking becomes a challenge; hidden windfall and ground-level brush can become traps for the most agile people.

Landmarks that were easily recognizable weeks earlier are hidden under the cover of white.

In the woods, the wine-like aroma of the duff on a warm fall day is only a memory. Smells are limited to those brought forth by chain saws and fresh sawdust. Trying to draw in new scents only brings icy-cold air that presents a freezing feeling to sinuses.

The woods tell us winter has arrived through the stillness that prevails. Animal tracks tell of activity and movement, but the chill has limited even the animals so commonly seen during fall.

With the stillness comes a wonderful quietness understood only by those who have taken time to stop and appreciate its effect. The quietness magnifies every pop and snap made by the otherwise motionless trees.

Those who have carried a saw into the woods have learned well the story of winter in the woods. They've worked hard to cope with the cold, stinging wet hands

Roaming the Roads of Rural Life

created by snow-covered wood. They've tried to find the fine balance of clothing required to not become too warm and yet not too cold.

Winter in the woods brings about a new appreciation for many simple things in life, too. It makes us appreciate dry clothes and the warmth found with family at home after the shortness of a December day had been turned into a long day of working in the harsh cold.

Winter in the woods makes us better appreciate how simple life can be outside the hustle and bustle of everyday life. Everything is broken down into the simplest of terms during that time in the woods.

I long for that sort of simplicity, as I long for each of the few times I ever get to visit the Veefkind woods on winter days.

I long for the times when I can depend on the woods to tell me "winter is here."

Beauty in Sight Only

The snow looked edible. The snow looked warming.

The snow was a combination of cotton candy and fiber that can be made into clothing as it hung on the limbs of bushes and trees in the woods.

It was easy to see those things from the comfort of my favorite stump as I looked around the woods. I'd seen the snow take such a form in the bushes and trees before, and I've seen it many times since.

I'm far from certain about what conditions make it perfect for snow to form into large snowballs as it catches in those limbs. I've seen it on warm mornings; I've seen it on cold mornings.

My mind drifted to thoughts of how Willie Wonka, that wonderfully quirky fictional candy maker, would have viewed that day's winter splendor. He'd have seen sweetness in puffy pieces of candy – maybe even sweeter than any cotton candy the snow was mimicking.

My mind drifted to the value the snow would bring if I could pluck its puffs from the limbs and have them woven into clothing, which could add to the layers of warmth-saving cloth that were covering my body that day.

So often, it's easy to see such sweetness and warmth in the snow. We want to surround ourselves in it; we want to roll in it and slide on it. We want to jump into piles of it; we want to rub it onto our skin.

But the snow has a side that's deceiving to our eyes. That brightness and all the other visions can bring the harsh side of snow's personality.

Even those cotton candy-like puffs hanging on the limbs could, in an instant, shake me into the reality of that harshness. All it takes is a simple stroll through that brush to feel the mischief of the snow.

Walk under that tree and a gust of icy wind knocks one of the puffs from the tree's limbs and onto your hat.

Duck under some of the wood's thick brush and a puff falls from the limbs and onto the back of your neck.

It's on your head; it's fallen down the back of your neck and between the cool shell of your clothing and the warm skin of your back.

The snow in my woods – or for that matter, in any woods – isn't sweet. It's freezing and bland.

That snow doesn't keep you warm, except in the warmth its sight brings to your heart.

People who understand snow know to look, but don't touch – and don't bother to taste. We allow our minds to trick us into thinking the best things about cottony snow hanging in limbs might be something deeper than anything a lifetime of learning about it has taught.

Games Played with the Moon's Brightness

The moon's game of hide-and-seek lasted only for an hour or so.

In the game, the moon peeked from behind clouds just long enough to spur on a rural sky-watcher's interest. Its brightness illuminated the thawing earth as a spotlight might brighten a performing star's presence.

It was the first sign of spring's arrival – a sign far beyond any provided by a migrating bird or a creature emerging from hibernation.

The clouds behind the moon's game were clouds only in the sense that they were opaque. Those clouds resulted from fog rising from the day's late-winter sun, which had bored its force into the earth and mixed with the cement-like frost – a frost that the sun soon would pull from the soil.

I associate the full moon with fall harvests; seeing it glow above freshly harvested cornfields and serving as a harbinger of the winter that will follow.

On this night, however, the full moon represented the annual struggle between the dead cold of winter and the penetrating warmth that soon would make the trees bud and pump green life back into the grass.

The struggle continued with every dip the moon made behind the low-hanging clouds.

Is spring really here? The moon would glow in its fullness to reply with a resounding "yes!"

Is spring really here? A third of the moon would glow from over the top of the fog and reply with a muffled "mmmmmmmaybe!"

Is spring really here? The moon would disappear behind the fog's deceiving thickness and answer with a distant "noooooooo!"

The process repeated itself over and over until a grown man, who always will be a rural youngster, might become lost in what even that night might bring, much less worry about whether tomorrow would be a winter coat or a tee-shirt day. Time and experience will tell him it won't help to worry about those sorts of things; whatever tomorrow brings, tomorrow brings.

Experience also will tell the youngster that, even if spring weather isn't there the next day, it will be there the day after that – and, if not then, the next day. He will understand the late-winter moon, playing its game of hide-and-seek behind the fog, is all the sign he will need to know that the time for warmth has arrived.

In between, there will be wet feet and fingers feeling the stinging numb of winter's cold. There will be times of dressing too lightly and times of dressing too warmly. There will be the smell of maple syrup cooking and the smells of cow manure melting on the fields.

There will be daydreams of fishing along the riverbank on a sunny summer day. There will be hopes that planting will be done cleanly and quickly and that every seed will produce greatly.

There will be mud. There will be much mud.

In a few days, warm nights will peel away the fog that so effectively served as cover during the moon's game. The day's sun will have evened out the earth's temperature between the days and nights.

In a few days, we probably will have forgotten the moon's game of hide-and-seek and will have moved on to listening to the frogs chirping and the loons calling.

But for that late-winter night, I chose to direct a knowing wink and a nod toward the sky, in honor of the way the moon introduced me to spring in such a quiet and peaceful manner.

Spring Will Win the Fight

Spring wins again.

It's never been a contest, really. But, somehow, I and many others feel a twinge of depression whenever a winter storm forces its way into our lives, about the time we should be thinking more about flying kites and leprechauns dancing across lush, spring green pastures.

It seems there haven't been too many years of my middle-aged life when spring hasn't teased us in February and early March, only to have a good amount of snow fall on the once-bared earth.

The old-timers generally are good at rationalizing the March snow phenomenon. They say things like "it has to snow three times on the robins' backs before spring – or was that four times?" Or, you might hear an older fella talk about the number of times he's shoveled snow on Mother's Day.

A late-winter walk around the woods reminded me how it doesn't matter what the old-timers – or any of us, for that matter – say about snow and the coming of spring. The fact, plain and simple, is the calendar hit "spring," and that's the way it is.

Whether we got a snowfall or two before or after the first day of spring really doesn't matter. It's not winter and, no matter how deep the drifts which are left behind, spring is here.

The trees in my woods "talked" to me about spring while I took a break during my leisurely stroll. I'm apt to wind up in a near-prone position against the south side of an old oak or maple tree during such midday walks, and the warmth collected by the trees spoke louder than any creature in the woods.

"Spring is here!" the trees called.

Never mind the 6 inches of snow on the ground from a storm that passed through the day before. The sun's drumming on the south side of the trees had made short work of whatever snow was hanging on those trees, and was working swiftly on the snow around the trees' bases.

I knew this hadn't been a December or January snowstorm, which would have been followed by days short on sun and nights long on bitter cold. That snow is allowed by the tilt of the earth to stay around for a month or two.

But, not this snow. This snow would be gone in a day or two.

This snow would be seeping into the earth, preparing the fields around the woods for spring planting. It wouldn't be long before the machinery would rumble across the fields.

Mothers soon would remind their children to remove shoes and boots carrying mud from spring farmyard excursions.

Children, young and old, would soon spend time in pastures and woodlots, gazing at puffy clouds and daydreaming.

Those things, and so much more that comes to life with spring, are just around the corner, the trees said.

Winter and its cold bite can try as they may, but this is no contest. Winter is gone, and spring is here.

Spring wins again.

Spring's Arrival on the Wing

The calendar says today is the first day of spring, but I think it arrived last week.

There have been plenty of signs of spring's arrival – the melting snow, the sounds of basketball tournaments echoing from televisions. However, the greatest sign was sounded while I took a short walk into a stand of young pine trees. I didn't even have to take the longer walk into the large woods a bit farther away to find telltale signs that rivers would soon be running strongly and gurgling gently everywhere around me.

Sparrows chirped loudly in the small pines that day, but one chirp in particular caught my ear. I stopped and listened for what I'd thought I'd heard, but for a few minutes could only hear the chattering sparrows.

I started walking and soon heard what I'd thought I'd heard earlier. Again, I listened closely and heard the unmistakable sharp chirp and song of a redwing blackbird.

The redwing's voice pierced through the sparrows' noise, sounding a voice of reason for the spring.

It took a few moments for me to follow the redwing's song so my eyes could confirm what my ears were telling me. My eyes found it perched in a tree across a small opening in the trees, where the redwing seemed to be lonely among the trees and sparrows. But the redwing was there, all the same.

The reason for my excitement at seeing the redwing blackbird is that redwings don't fool around when it comes to the heralding of spring. When redwings arrive, you can count on the arrival of warm weather, melting snow and ice break-ups.

My excitement for seeing the redwings' arrival is a bit tempered, since their habitat is threatened by development. I took a moment to say a quick prayer that development will never overtake Veefkind's wetlands, so at least there the redwings will continue to provide me with their unique signaling of spring.

Some folks contend that the appearance of robins is a definite sign of spring in our northern climes. But I often challenge northern people to think back to how many times they've seen a robin weathering a blizzard – a puffed out ball of brown and orange, covered with snow and likely wondering why it made such a foolishly premature visit.

A redwing, on the other hand, never seems to show itself until people have been fully infected with cabin fever.

A redwing is much like a person on the rural route – neither is foolhardy. When the redwings arrive, people start thinking about planting crops and gardens, fishing, and pulling out the old tent.

How many redwing blackbirds have ever been spotted weathering a snowstorm?

There are some other sure signs of spring – things like the songs of meadowlarks and the barking calls of geese overhead.

Surprise spring snowstorms are the rule in these parts, but as I stood and looked at the redwing blackbird in that small stand of pine trees, I had a good feeling that winter really was over. And, if the redwing's arrival had been another of those false harbingers of spring, I'll at least have had the chance to appreciate the year's first redwing blackbird sighting.

Within days, I knew there would be thousands of redwings chattering there in preparation for the coming nesting season. But none is ever as warming as the first redwing that called across the opening to tell me spring had arrived.

The Spring Songs of Frogs

The air outside is still brisk at night, which hasn't yet made it conducive to having windows open at night for the sake of allowing fresh air into the house.

One of the windows was flung open at my house, though, when I thought I heard a telltale chirping going on outside.

The house had been quiet and I was curled up with a book when I heard the first frogs croaking outside. I jumped from my chair and dashed across the room to the nearest window and threw it open.

There was a moment when I felt like the young boy who'd opened the window and threw up the sash when he heard Santa and his reindeer on the roof. But unlike that boy, I didn't hear what I'd expected to hear as I leaned on the windowsill. No frogs were croaking. No reindeer were clacking on the roof, either.

There was silence under the stars on that moonless night.

The crisp air felt good on my face and in my lungs, so I spent some moments at the window, taking in the feeling of newness that such an early spring night can bring. As I stood there, I realized that the sound of the window slamming open would have caught any frog's attention and caused it to stop chirping.

After a few minutes, my patience and suspicion paid dividends. There was a chirp in the distance; there was an answering chirp. Others joined, mostly with chirping, but with some deep-throated croaking adding harmony.

I closed my eyes and listened. Spring had arrived in Veefkind.

Besides any memories the sound of the frogs might bring to me – memories of youth camping adventures or of visits to my grandparents' house, where the frogs always seemed to be singing – they signal the hurry-scurry pace that warm weather brings. It makes you realize that you will have to get the old lawn mower out in a couple of weeks unless you want the buzz of mosquitoes to make more noise than the frogs.

Seemingly every weekend will mean something will be going on somewhere, the frogs seem to say.

"Let the window stay open, because you'll need it open for the coming hot weather," they seemed to be telling me.

Frogs have it good in hot weather, because they get to stay in the cool water while they catch those nasty mosquitoes.

Listening to the frogs can be an experience in itself. One frog alone hardly makes noise, but when they're multiplied by the thousands, they can get pretty loud. That's not too bad if you listen to them in passing, but the sound can overtake your senses if you concentrate on it for a while.

I was lucky to not be living so close to a swamp that the frogs would make me feel as though they were going to overrun the house at any time. It was that way at my grandparents' house when, as a young boy, I visited them. I didn't understand the frogs much as a little guy; the frogs sounded like they were all around me during those visits.

The frogs made me curious; sometimes too curious for their own good.

Somebody told me once that frog legs taste good, so my friend Ken and I caught as many as we could in one afternoon and put them into a tank at home. The plan was to sell them to local restaurants; maybe even to sample a few of their bouncy legs ourselves.

We put boards into the tanks for the creatures to sit on, and they made short work of getting out of the tank by jumping off the boards and over the edge of the tank. I guess I wasn't supposed to have the frogs, according to Mother Nature – maybe the critters knew what was in store for them.

The frogs made their noise every night since that night when I listened to them from the window. Their song compelled me to take a seat on my back steps to listen to their chorus a few nights later. I stayed until the chill drove me back into the house.

From inside the house, I knew that the frogs eventually would pull the heat of summer to Veefkind, and that I'd soon be listening to their yapping through an open window while I waited for the beautiful cool of the next fall.

A Good Place for Purification

The container touted its contents as "pure."

"How can anything that comes from a tree be pure?" my friend asked, as he turned the maple syrup container to find other content information.

It was one of those questions that didn't really require an answer, and one the friend didn't really expect to be answered. It was just one of those questions asked between friends when there wasn't much else to talk about.

Still, I thought about the question as I strolled through the woods at Veefkind.

It was a gloomy afternoon, and the grass – still matted from the snow – and the trees were dripping from steady drizzle that fell earlier in the day. I sat on a stump to take in the spring sights, smells and sounds which, in the woods, are second only to those sensed in the fall.

The wetness on the trees seemed to be especially heavy on a tree that had limbs hanging over my stump. Droplets fell onto me at a near-steady pace.

When I looked up to see what made the tree wetter than others around it, I was surprised to see a broken-off branch. The branch was the source of the dripping, allowing sweet-tasting sap to drip onto my face as I looked up.

As I reached my tongue to lick the new-fallen sap from near my mouth, I thought about how the woods really is full of impurities, yet is so pure.

It seemed inevitable that a creature of some sort was nearby, probably carrying a disease that could infect other creatures of its kind.

Maybe a deer tick, laced with Lyme disease, lay in the grass near me, waiting to feast on my blood.

Or, one of the many molds or fungi growing there could somehow infect me and cause me great pain.

For that matter, the very tree that dripped its sweetness onto me could itself be "impure," by dropping one of its branches onto my head.

Even with its impurities, the woods is among the purest places I've ever known.

I knew the rain that fell that morning was seeping through generations of duff, cleansing the water of anything bad which had been collected as it passed through the air.

Whatever impurities had been contained in the leaves and grass was being broken down by the soil's own chemicals and bacteria.

I knew the leaves which would soon spring from the buds forming on the branches would be flushing filth from the air and pouring life-giving oxygen into the world.

Thousands of similar purifying actions were taking place that day in the woods.

The actions also included my tree with the broken branch having used its own natural abilities to cleanse its sugars and liquids, and allow them to ooze in a pure form from the branch.

It became clear that, in a place with such purifying effects, it shouldn't be surprising how syrup producers may refer to their product as "pure."

The thoughts of the woods' impurities led me to realize, above all, it has a purifying affect on me.

My senses are cleared when I'm there; everything becomes clear and real in the woods.

Troubles and worries are lost somewhere in the bark of trees surrounding me.

Anyone who's ever taken time to allow some "pure" maple syrup to drip onto them understands.

Where the Stars Shine Brightly

The stars were bright as I stood outside my truck, gazing at them one evening at Veefkind.

There seemed to be too many of the stars to even make out some of the most well-known constellations – a fact that didn't surprise me, because I generally have trouble picking out much more than the Big Dipper. The Milky Way brightened a path through the stars on that moonlit night, adding to the aura of stars that are unimaginable numbers of miles away from the spot where I was standing on that gravel road.

I'd made the stop on purpose. I wanted to know if there was truth in something I'd heard a few days earlier.

The question I had was about words I'd heard at the Einstein Theater at the Smithsonian Air and Space Museum in Washington D.C. There, a young man described what people might see for stars in that night's sky.

The show in the theater started with the lights turned down and with a projector shooting images of that night's sky onto the theater's ceiling-screen. At the start, I thought the show wasn't going to be worth the price of admission. The projected stars were difficult to make out, because of the light that remained in the room.

The projectionist was quick to say he was showing the sort of sky we might expect to see in the Washington metropolitan area. Then, he completely turned off the room's lights to present a better picture of the stars.

"This is the sky that very few people get to see," he said as the room darkened and the projected stars sparkled on the ceiling.

I welcomed the darkness. I was deeply interested in the program, but a long day of walking in the city and a schedule that allowed little sleep for three previous nights had the darkness make me consider a nap.

But, my attention returned to the program with the projectionist's next words.

"We *all* live where there's so much light pollution from street lights that you may never see the sky this way," he said.

My eyes opened and I rose in my reclined seat.

I wanted to blurt out to him that, along my rural routes, the sky most certainly is just like the one he was saying none of us would see. I'd spent many hours under my rural sky, gazing at its zillions of stars and planets. I'd photographed meteorite showers that criss-crossed the starlight. I'd peered at them with my son, Jamie, lying on our backs and using an identification wheel that we'd purchased at a science museum – we did our best to identify a few constellations.

The beauty of the Milky Way, which cuts the bright path through moonless nights, has brought many hours of wonder into my home.

But, they don't get to see that sky in Washington – or in so many other cities – because those people choose to live every night under city lights.

My stop along the roadside at Veefkind didn't last long. It was a little too cold to drop my truck's tailgate and lay back in the box to spend a few hours gazing at the stars. I would return there another time to fully appreciate my unlit night sky.

Short of sounding selfish, I realize there are many other rural areas where the stars can be seen as well as I can see them at Veefkind. And, unlike the young fellow at the Einstein Theater, I can tell people that there are plenty of us on rural routes who can see the stars and who take time to stop and look at the sky.

Maybe the best thing we could do, though, is to keep the beautiful sky as one of our rural secrets. If too many people know about our sky, they're bound to come to join us – and, probably bring plenty of that ugly light pollution with them.

Feeling Freedom in a New Pasture

I stopped my truck along a country road one recent June morning to watch a group of heifers just released into a new pasture.

Heifers such as those do well expressing what a June morning in a new patch of grass is all about, I've always thought. They spin and kick like bucking broncos, all seeming to want to outdo the others in their animal-level display of joy.

Dew flew from those heifers' hooves as they tore around the pasture grasses lush as only they could be in early June.

The heifers made me think of the number of times I've watched children escape the bounds of their schoolrooms during so many Junes; their youthful exuberance evident as they did their own versions of "kicking up their heels" while running, screaming and yelling in delight.

Many country children have known, over the years, that they soon would have the chance to be in that same pasture grass, right where their farms' heifers had been shown freedom.

Plenty of country people learned at an early age how good a stem of newly grown dew-covered pasture grass would feel and taste. Its sweetness gushes from the stem as it's rolled between molars in a fashion not so dissimilar to the way the heifers chew after they've settled into grazing on the lush herbal carpet.

The number of times I've felt the joy of chewing such a stem of grass on a June morning made me wonder: Is it just the sweetness of the grass that makes me long to be in that pasture, enjoying the grass with those heifers?

It was that small herd's excitement that made me realize why we all love to walk in those pastures during June. I realized why it's so enjoyable to be rolling the stem of grass in my mouth.

The pasture, though surrounded by a fence, represents much more than a taste of the best grass nature can offer. More than anything, it represents the freedom of the open countryside; the freedom of a youngster springing from the confining space of a school classroom to breathe the crisp air of an Upper Midwest morning.

Sure, there's plenty of work to do during the summer. And, like the fence around the pasture, there are certain boundaries in which we still will be expected to stay.

But, we know the pasture brings with it some idle time; some time to collect our thoughts and examine our own human condition.

That's a good enough reason for any creature to bound across a pasture, kicking up heels in a bit of joy during a June morning.

We may not display it the same way it was displayed by those heifers, or by those country children who'd longed so much for the freedom of summer. It might only be within our hearts, the feeling of "kicking up our heels" in such a pasture, but isn't that where it counts the most, anyway?

It's sad, in a way, that more people haven't felt the joy a new pasture can bring to them – even for some who have actually entered a pasture on a June morning but who haven't really understood its significance.

While we can have sadness within us for those poor souls who don't know the new pasture's feeling, it won't stop those of us who have *felt* the pasture from getting out of the truck to join the heifers in their exuberance.

It won't stop me from wanting to step onto many more fresh pastures. Each time I do, I'll feel the excitement shown by the heifers, and all the excitement felt by school children who realize the summer is theirs to enjoy.

A Rocky Conversation

"I don't know why people would want to decorate with rocks," Dad said as we sat in my car on a toasty summer afternoon. "I think they're ugly."

It took me a moment to snap out of the daze I'd fallen into while waiting for the stoplight to change. As I did, I questioned my father about why he felt that way. The rocks being used on a nearby landscaping job did a nice job of complementing the terrain, it seemed to me.

At least, that's what I thought before Dad reminded me about rocks.

"They'd never want to put rocks in their front yard like that if they picked as many of them as I have over the years," he said.

I think I knew what he was talking about, but only to a certain extent. There was rock-picking done while I grew up on our farm, but nothing like the rock-picking he talked about happening a generation earlier.

The rock-picking I knew was the kind where a few "grew" in the fields every spring. Most of them weren't much bigger than a large potato, but they would easily have been big enough to do serious damage to the knives on the old Gehl forage chopper.

The rock-picking Dad spoke about had to do with fields that hadn't been cleared of brush too long before his youth. There were plenty of surprises in those kinds of fields; rock surprises requiring an afternoon's work for the big ones to be moved. Some were so big that people just plowed around them.

Dad's idea of decorating with rocks was having a large pile somewhere in the cow yard or using them to fill empty foundations of old buildings.

We talked about the dozens of other constructive uses for rocks we've seen over the years: like the rock fences in some areas of Wisconsin or the rocks we've seen used as siding for many Wisconsin homes.

People who find the more constructive uses – translated to mean someone found ways to make money by selling things to other people – call them things like "fieldstones." In Veefkind, we've never bothered much with the fancier names. To us, those hard round things from the field are pretty much still "rocks" or "stones."

The folks who landscaped the lawn Dad critiqued had ideas of making the lawn look more natural by setting a few bigger rocks around the yard. Maybe they wanted something for the neighborhood kids to hop over as they passed through the yard.

I'd like to believe somebody was thinking about using such decorations as memorials to the toil so many farm kids completed at one time or another. "Picking rocks," it seems, is only romantic when you look back at the work from many years hence; even then, most of us think those aren't such great memories.

Or, more likely, the landscapers put the rocks in their place to see whether some old fella and his quirky, aging son would someday strike up a conversation over such inanimate objects.

June Mornings Don't Last Forever

The trip I'd made across the open grassland on a recent morning at Veefkind was a necessary one.

At its completion, I momentarily wished that I'd waited until later in the day to make that trip. The tall grasses on that open area of land carried the glistening dew of a sunny Wisconsin morning in June.

It seemed that much of that dew had been transferred to the legs of my jeans, which were dew-soaked from mid-

Rural Routes & Ruts

thigh to the tops of my shoes. With every step, my shoes gushed with the squishy-squashy sounds of the wetness.

The grass had left many of its seeds on those wet jeans – seemingly enough to seed down a field that would feed a 50-cow dairy herd through a winter.

It was a feeling for which I had no liking as a youngster. It was one that had often left me chilled in the morning air after a trip down the lane to drive our cows to their pasture.

It was one of those feelings that brought back memories of childhood; the ones that carry some romantic feel, but which also have plenty of harsh realities.

As I pondered my situation on that recent morning, I almost laughed at myself for having forgotten the results of rushing through that grass. I considered how fewer and fewer people experience that feeling these days, guessing that decreasing farm numbers and changes in agricultural technology will leave even fewer chances for future generations to experience that sort of misery.

There are few reasons for anyone these days to be dashing through dew-covered tall-grass meadows.

Even bearing the weight of the wet jeans and wet shoes, there came some pleasant memories of chasing the cows through that wet grass.

The most obvious is having the chance to drink in the fresh, sometimes crisp, morning air. There's something special about Wisconsin's June morning air that can't be matched at any other time during the day. It's been cleansed by the darkness, much as the darkness brings sleep that revitalizes us so that we might get through another day.

In the morning, the air hasn't been polluted by the smell of dust stirred by cars traveling down a gravel road or by any other smells. Even the smells of wildflowers can be subdued during that time, waiting for the approaching midday to create their strongest fragrances.

Nor has the air yet been polluted by many of the day-to-day sounds piercing the rural silence later in the day – planes passing overhead, tractors in the fields, vehicles whirring down nearby highways.

As I searched my mind for more pleasantries, I remembered the sweet taste of the grasses I found along my morning route. The sight of a farm kid chewing on a piece of grass might seem cliché to some, but most who have followed cows down a lane at some time or another have tasted the sweetness of having an early-summer piece of timothy in their mouth.

Many also have known the spectacular taste carried by a bud of red clover and the race with bees to grab a few of those buds before the bees started their morning pollination routes.

All of those feelings come during a short period; from the misery of walking home in wet jeans and wet shoes, to the fresh quiet air and on to the taste of the grasses. If it was going to be experienced, it needed to be experienced during a June morning.

A little sooner, and the grasses and air wouldn't be ripe enough; a few weeks later and it all will be over-ripe.

I decided then that much of what we experience in life comes with good and bad, much as the misery of that cold wetness went with the joys found by a child walking cattle to their pasture.

And, it all comes in what I've come to realize is a small window of opportunity.

As a youngster, it seemed those early June days might last forever. But, looking back at them, those days were here and gone in the relative blink of an eye.

Making my way through that wet morning grass on that recent June morning may not have been such a bad thing after all. It certainly served as a reminder that I should make the best of my opportunity to have another good day.

The memories of being a youngster following cattle through the dew-covered grass made me remember how short life really is, and how I need to make the most of every moment. Like the freshness of those June mornings, it really doesn't last long at all.

Fully Exposed to Life

I walked naked in the woods today.

The walk wasn't made for any profound purpose, or to seek any of the answers about life as many a person from the 1960s might do. Instead, the walk was made for pure utility purposes: to get to a camp shower that earlier in the day I'd hung on a tree near my camp.

I had no fear of being spotted by a passerby. No person of sound mind would have been wandering through or watching in any way in that remote wooded area – the location of which I'll carry as a secret all the way to my grave.

The walk was the simple result of the convenience of undressing at my camp. I would have a quick, cold shower of lake water from the camp shower-bag that hung from the tree. Then, I'd head directly back to my camp to sit beside a fire and warm up with a cup of coffee or tea.

It seemed such a utilitarian notion, making that walk to the shower and back. But the intensity of the walk surprised me. Literally baring myself to nature was itself a release, a feeling that I actually belonged as part of the natural world.

In my state of undress, I wasn't judged on the clothes I wore or by any social status. I, for a few magic minutes, was simply another creature of God's making.

Even better, though, was the feeling I got from the soft forest duff under my feet. It took a few moments of barefoot walking to realize that, in nearly 50 years of life, I'd never felt forest duff under my bare feet. Many times I'd scooped it up into my hands and many times I'd smelled it. I'd read its poetry and I'd written about it, but I'd never felt the duff's softness caressing the soles of my feet.

I worried for a moment that something might poke through and jab into one of my feet. Those fears disappeared through the knowledge that most of the sharp objects that could damage my feet would have been man-made – and, there hadn't been too many humans tossing junk into my special remote area.

Never had I felt the earth so reach into my being, making me feel like one of the billions of plants that thrive in places like this.

The duff's feel made me, in a way, a new spring plant.

So much of the rural world makes me feel renewal, and the feeling of new forest growth and the earth itself doubled the speed of that renewal.

I'll return often to that spot of renewal and hope that few others ever discover it. There, I may not bare my entire being to the woods, but I'll be sure to allow the duff to push its life-giving energy into the soles of my bare feet.

The Wonder of Nothing

There was only the sound of thunder and rain pattering on the roof early the other morning.

Usually at that magic time, just before daybreak, the noisy robins take to song to wake the world. However, they were quiet as the rain fell, letting the bouncing drops lull many people back to sleep.

Aside from the rain, there was nothing to listen to on that morning. And in its own way, even the noise the rain made on the roof was itself "nothing."

Raindrops are good at absorbing other sounds that might otherwise be heard on days when there is no rain. A vacuum seems to form as they suck the sky into the soil, cleaning the annoyance of human-generated noise just as it washes pollen and dust from the air. Maybe other sounds are being made – people talking, dogs barking, motors running, airplanes passing overhead – but when the clouds open, I've seldom heard anything but the raindrops slapping against the soil, or against the leaves or on a roof.

I've come to be able to pick out the sound of individual drops as they reach whatever it is that makes them explode into many pieces. If I'm lucky enough to be in a place where I can hear them hitting the roof over me, I close my eyes and imagine the drops massaging my temples and scalp, then whispering relaxing words into my ear.

When that happens, the massaging and whispering help me go where the concerns are few; where the finest sounds no longer are sounds at all. Nothing seems to matter in that place – I'm really able to hear "nothing."

Sometimes, listening to nothing is a good thing. It sort of allows you to clear your faculties.

Someone reminded me of that a while back, when he came up with the profound comment that he gets up early in the morning to listen to and see "nothing." His statement came after a visitor to his lake shack said there was nothing to see or hear that time of the day – and my friend said that's exactly what he gets up to hear and see.

Really, I suppose, you could imagine a lot of things that there are to see and hear just as the sun is peeking over the eastern horizon. The activity among animals is amazing at that time of the day, with the robins singing the world awake and the cows starting to get active.

Of course, to me, there is nothing that matches the early-morning activity of loons calling their eerie cries. That's a good addition to listening to nothing; their calls crack the early morning haze that generally hangs low on lakes.

The problem with listening to the loons on many lakes, however, is their calls usually are answered by the roar of outboard motors propelling people out for some early morning fishing.

Cows bellering to be milked can be a good or a bad sound to wake up with, depending on whether you like the work associated with having to roll out of bed to satisfy them. I guess it's an easier sound to endure if you know you don't have to pay them an official visit before you've even spoken with another human.

A favorite morning "nothing" activity for me, as with so many others I know, is sitting in a place where I can see the first glow of the morning sun sneaking over the horizon. That sort of light is revitalizing and makes me feel as though I really can be part of the coming day.

An expert photographer I once knew said pictures taken at sunrise are better than those taken at sunset because of some special sort of qualities of the morning's light rays. That seems to be true, but I think the photos taken in the morning are best because that's when the photographer has a new outlook on life – and therefore is a little more creative than during other times of the day.

As with the other morning's rainfall though, there are times when just hearing the patter of the rain on the roof is best for seeing and hearing "nothing" early in the morning. For me, the gurgling of a coffee maker would be about the only sound I wouldn't mind hearing with the rain – I so enjoy sipping my coffee with the rain falling.

The saddest part of enjoying such wonderful "nothingness" is that it's always so short-lived and quickly switches to the normal pace of the daily grind. People call for your attention; switches are flipped on machines to start relentless whirring, humming and banging.

Even when the day's "nothing" becomes "something," I always hope to find solace in remembering there's always the next morning. With some good fortune, the next morning will again bring the sound of raindrops on the roof and will be the wondrous noise of nothing that wakes me.

Nights of Rural Route Drama

The steamy summer night was still as I looked out of my bedroom window.

At first I didn't know why I was awake, or exactly what had drawn me to the window. But after a few seconds, I realized the culprit that called me there was an owl hooting in the front yard.

The big bird was making plenty of noise, and there was little I could do about it – even closing the window wasn't an option, since the house didn't have air conditioning and the heat and humidity was nearly suffocating. I simply lay back down to try to get some sleep.

There was little sleep to be had, however, because the owl's hooting was joined by the hoots of an owl somewhere in the distance. They seemed to start their own mini-drama with their conversation.

"Who who who whoooooo," the nearby owl said.

"Whoooooo whoooooo whoooooo," the distant owl answered.

Time after time they went through their conversation, alternating the lengths of each hoot to provide any imaginable combination of owl talk.

It wasn't only their incessant noise that kept me awake. I also lay staring into the room's moonlit darkness, thinking about what the owls could possibly be saying that was important enough to keep me awake for so long.

Sleep eventually overtook me despite the loud conversation going on outside.

The owls were long gone for the day when I woke in the morning. After a few minutes, the short-lived silence was broken by the final gurgles of my coffee maker and the blaring of a morning television news broadcast.

Sorting through the new noise, I listened to a newscaster talk about a vigilante who had been arrested. The vigilante had shot some hoodlums in a subway in his attempt to single-handedly clean up some subway crime.

My mind shifted back to the previous night and wondered why the owls had chosen that night to keep me awake with the conversation in my front yard; I had so much to do that day.

I suspected one of the owls was one I'd seen recently inhabiting my woods. Mixed emotions had welled in me when I saw the big bird. I knew it deserved a respectful place in nature's scheme and that it was ridding us of pests like mice. But I also knew it would damage the year's rabbit population, leaving my trusty beagle and me with fewer chances to sharpen our rabbit-chasing skills.

Maybe it was the owl that had recently scared the wits out of me when it swooped in front of my car's headlights as I drove past a nearby woods.

My attention flicked back to the newscaster, who continued to yap about the rights and wrongs of having a vigilante cleaning up crime on a subway.

Thoughts about the subway lingered as I poured my second cup of coffee. With my mood soured by my lack of sleep, I wondered whether my balky car would start. I knew that if I lived in the comfort of a city, at least I could walk to work or to a subway ride if the car didn't start. Maybe a neighbor would even be able to pick me up on his way to work if I lived in a city, I thought, as the newscaster reported for the fifth time the condition of the four youths who were shot by the vigilante.

The newscaster said there was plenty of public support for the vigilante. People didn't seem to have a problem with a man defending himself from four younger males who were terrorizing him for $5.

I poured a third cup of coffee as the newscaster finished his report about the vigilante. My car, which had started with the first crank of its starter, was idling in the driveway. And the two previous cups of coffee had melted away some of the irritation caused by my lost sleep.

Finally, the night I'd spent with those noisy owls was contrasted with the night I could have been spending in a city.

The owls' hoots were soothing compared with the racket of city traffic that could have been keeping me awake at night.

It was better for an owl to startle me by swooping into my headlights than to have to worry about people jumping from sidewalks into my car's path.

It was better to worry about owls swooping onto rabbits rather than feeling like a rabbit as I got onto a subway, wondering if that day there would be a human "owl" dressed as a mugger swooping down onto me.

A smile crossed my face as I headed out to the car, having realized that living along a rural route for so long had spoiled me. After a while, it's easy to lose perspective when daily worries don't involve big-city life-and-death drama; when daily worries become whether the old car will start and whether hooting owls will interrupt a night's sleep.

That morning, I drove to work smiling, looking forward to the next night's dramatic conversations between two owls.

Hummingbirds in a World of Eagles

I watched a colorful little hummingbird use its needle-like beak to draw nectar from a vibrant flower.

A measure of pity crossed my mind for the little creature as I saw it working. The tiny bird had nowhere to perch as it performed its work; work so vital because the energy drawn from the nectar was needed to give life to the creature. I wanted badly for that little bird to succeed so it could be there for me to see on another day, yet I knew how much energy it was taking for the bird to be there and how much nectar it would need to find for it to return for more nectar.

The bird, I knew, was trapped within its own circular struggle of finding its way to survival.

In the past year, I'd also watched eagles drift above Alaska's rivers. I'd seen them coast and swoop so smoothly – so effortlessly – from the sky to snatch fish from the rivers.

I'd also seen a small bundle of fur lying in an opening within a Wisconsin woods. I knew it was the leftovers from the previous night, when an owl had made a silent attack on a rabbit. I knew that, covered in darkness, the owl had used the advantage given by its specially-adapted feathers to drop – seemingly effortlessly – from its perch to make a meal of the rabbit.

Along a roadside, I'd watched as a red-tailed hawk floated, floated, floated, in the sky before it raised its wings high above its body to effortlessly pierce the air on the way to capturing a field mouse.

So little effort, it seems, was made by those eagles, that owl and that hawk.

When people tell each other to "spread your wings and fly," visions of those eagles, that owl and that hawk so easily come to mind. We want to be able to sustain ourselves with such effortless flight – soaring, coasting and diving, all so silently and with such ease.

So often I'd longed to be one of them, allowing a light summer breeze to lift my wings as I oversaw the wonders of our Upper Midwest countryside.

But I suspect that most of us are more like that little hummingbird: spreading our wings and finding the life-sustaining nectar that makes us who we are requires endless energy – sometimes life-draining energy.

Like the hummingbirds, our wings pound thousands of beats every minute; they hum and buzz as we reach for our versions of nectar. The energy pours from our bodies as we search and then hover as we draw nearer to our prize.

The energy, we find, is sometimes difficult to muster as we make our hummingbird-like attempts to spread our wings. But when we reach the nectar, we realize that we've accomplished our feat just as those eagles, that owl and that hawk reached their goals.

The hummingbirds may not have the same majestic grace of an eagle, owl or hawk. But the hummingbirds, themselves so full of energy and color, are able to draw their sustenance from all that is so bright and colorful around us – something that may never be said for those birds that seem to soar so effortlessly.

The hummingbirds know all that is beautiful and sweet.

Rural Routes & Ruts

Chirp of the Crickets

My friend commented on how good the crickets were sounding that year and was surprised to hear me say I couldn't hear them.

Such a personal revelation was surprising to some of the people who surrounded me. Indeed, my friend insisted that I must have been joking, because the chirping was incessant and somewhat loud.

It was no surprise to me, but I was frightened. I was becoming a carbon copy of my father, able to hear most sounds and normal conversation, but missing the sounds of certain tones.

The malady wasn't inherited, I've believed. It was more likely the result of youthful days spent on loud tractors and generally working around other noisy equipment. Mine were the days when little, if any, attention was given to hearing protection when working around loud farm equipment, or when shooting shotguns or rifles in preparation for hunting.

Our ears would ring for a while when the loud noise stopped, or when we moved away from it. Sometimes a headache would linger for a while, but it was simply assumed to be a fact of life.

Many may not worry about such loss of a tone in their hearing. But I want to be able to hear the crickets.

The last time I heard them, the air was hanging heavily in the hot, early August air as I strolled down the old railroad right-of-way in my old Veefkind stomping grounds. The heat and humidity together was comparable to mid-summer afternoons that I've experienced on a South Pacific island or in South Carolina. And, while the humidity wasn't the same, the heat was comparable to any of the worst drought years at my central Wisconsin home.

But something I was still able to hear from the crickets back then told me that, as a lover of fall weather and the harvest season, I shouldn't be too worried that the day's weather was still good only for extended lunchtime naps under one of my family farm's old shade trees.

The chirping of those late-summer crickets made me take note of the soon-to-come change from the hot days of summer to those wonderful cool days of a Wisconsin fall.

I have no idea of what type of crickets those were, the ones that I longed to hear that day with my friend. Frankly, I don't care. I only knew they told me that those of us who still grew oats to its full ripeness should have been using the slack time provided by the dog days of summer to think about preparing the harvesting equipment, and patching that hole in the granary wall.

The sounds of those little bugs' rubbing legs also made me tend to remember my younger days – a time when dust from the oats and ragweed caused itching and sneezing that I fought in favor of catching grasshoppers that had made it alive through the combine used in the harvest and into the oats bin.

On a day such as my walk along the old railroad, the crickets' chirping might have occasionally been interrupted by the wild cackling of the hundreds of blackbirds I'd startled from their resting place among the rows of an adjacent cornfield.

Those blackbirds also have done well in serving as harbingers of summer's end, at least to me. I knew it would be a couple of weeks before those hundreds of birds would be flocking by the thousands and making their final calls that would be loud to me even later in life.

I've known some people who would envy me for no longer being able to hear the chirping crickets. Those body-conscious people who'd meant to work off a few pounds during the summer start to realize time's running out when the chirping starts. Water-lovers start to see nature take over what earlier in the spring and summer had been clear water, turning it into a green cesspool. The long, lush green grasses that serve as good chawin' material for kids would be going to seed – leaving aged grass that would be like chewing an oak twig.

But the chirping also has signaled the groaning sound made by an ear of sweet corn being husked and the sweet taste of the corn as it dripped with melted butter. The chirping would bring the gold and red of fall maples; the coming of cool evenings to offer relief from the sleeplessness of steamy summer nights.

I remember having considered stopping my August stroll that day while listening to the crickets, and finding refuge in a cool shower to rinse away the perspiration that had beaded on my forehead and dripped a stinging wetness into my eyes. But before I climbed into my truck to retreat to that relief, I stopped one last time to listen to the chirping crickets.

Their chirping made me realize I soon wouldn't have to worry about perspiration running into my eyes; instead I would take glee in selecting which flannel shirt to wear.

Maybe I'll never be able to hear the crickets again.

Maybe I'll have to search my other senses to serve as my signal for the coming end of summer.

But I'd like to join my friend in being able to hear the crickets, even on those nights when the stillness amplifies the chirping enough to keep all in the house from sleeping.

I want to be the one who asks my friend and others to join me in listening to the crickets with their message of the changing seasons.

Reflections of the Dog Days

They told me I couldn't go swimming down at the proverbial local swimming hole on those late days in July and August.

I wasn't certain why that was the rule in those times, other than whatever Dad said became a rule, and Dad definitely said, "Don't go swimming on those late days in July and August."

He called those days the "dog days of summer."

The local swimming hole, for us, was a place we called "Beels' Bridge." The bridge wasn't actually named after the Beels family – or owned by them – but the land on which we unquestioningly traipsed was, and still is, owned by the Beels family; a family which has lived for many years near my Veefkind home.

At Beels' Bridge, we gleefully shared the water of Wisconsin's Yellow River with some of the neighborhood dairy cattle.

At the time, it would have made sense to a youngster that the hottest days of summer were the best days to be cooling down in the river. Instead, we were relegated to staying home and doing chores which were put off during the planting season or while hay was being made. When there weren't chores, there was relaxation under the farm's shade trees or on the porch swing. And, when there was neither, there were neighborhood softball or football games played in the sweltering heat – games which, by day's end, left legs rubbery and clothes drenched with sweat under the sweltering sun and humidity.

We knew little about the bacteria, fungus or parasites growing in the water as summer's days started to grow just a bit shorter. All we knew was that plenty of green gunk started to grow on the water in the days leading up to the "dog days of summer."

I stopped my truck by Beels' Bridge and got out one August day, just to look over the bridge's railing and into the water below.

For a moment, I wished I'd followed Dad's instructions and never gone to the river that time of year. Before leaving, I'd even worried that his orders had little to do with our youthful health, but with what we might see there later in life.

The cows weren't there. They long since had been fenced closer to the farm's barnyard to keep them off the small river's banks and out of its channel.

The bridge is more modern than the large, steel structure that once stood above our summer gathering place. And, it didn't seem nearly as far from the bridge to the water as it once had seemed to a small boy following older siblings and neighbors to the swimming spot.

Worst of all, I could see my reflection in the murky water, even from the bridge.

The water seemed familiar. Its gentle flow made me feel every dip and every rock on the river's bottom; I knew the deepest spots, just as I'd known them 40 years earlier.

I remembered looking at my reflection from the bridge railing those many years earlier.

Despite its familiarity, I knew the river's flow had, in time, probably changed the channel. I understood such reality by looking at my aging reflection on the water's surface. There were many changes in the reflection and I remembered that, like the changes made by the moving water, time would continue to move and make still more changes in my reflection.

I wanted, for a moment, to jump into the water and do what I could to disrupt its flow for only a moment and change the way it seemed to affect my physical image. If nothing else, I thought a dip in the stream would do well in testing Dad's long-standing belief about not swimming that time of the year.

I vividly remembered the strength in Dad's words about not jumping into the river during the "dog days." It was one of the many things I'd learned from him. And, for a moment, I became angered that I'd never again hear him give such an admonishment. The years had flowed like the river and we'd buried him the previous spring in the nearby cemetery.

Still, the thought of how adamant he was about his "dog days" swimming rule brought a smile to my face and the satisfaction that, though not there physically, his words would continue to guide me in many ways.

Not much swimming goes on at swimming holes in small rivers and creeks these days. Perhaps young people fear someday looking at their reflection as I did that day at Beels' Bridge, able to see time passing so quickly, like the river during the short spells of heat in a Wisconsin summer.

Whether more generations care to risk looking into the murky water is up to them. The only thing for certain is, those of us who have taken the risk of seeing their reflection change in the water of such a place, will know to tell younger souls to never swim during the "dog days of summer."

Tenacititis Bolditriticus Stickinfinitum

They clung to the hood of my truck, those grasshoppers, and they just wouldn't let go.

One of my brothers had just been telling me the day before about the large numbers of grasshoppers invading his hay fields. I was seeing first-hand what he was talking about as I drove my truck back to the Veefkind woods.

The grasshoppers bounced all over the place as I drove through the tall grass of the lane that leads from the road to the woods. I had to roll up the windows so they didn't leap into the truck's cab; it seemed there were enough of them out there to push me out of the truck if they did make it in.

It was important that the windows were rolled up, because those little bouncers are so tenacious, they will do everything but pull open the door if they set their mind to it. Anyone who's ever been in an Upper Midwest farm field in August – especially combining oats – can agree.

The creatures probably have some sort of a Latin name – my limited research (looking in a single dictionary) tells me they're part of the order Saltatoria. If I were to create a

Latin-sounding name for grasshoppers, it would be something like Tenacititis Bolditriticus Stickinfinitum.

The Tenacititis refers to their tenacity. When they want to get somewhere, they simply tenaciously hang on and, well, they get there.

The Bolditriticus refers to how bold grasshoppers get. They don't care whether it's a plant, animal or machine or on what part they feel like landing. If it's a human eyeball that gets in their way, a grasshopper will jump onto it; if it's the grill of a fast-moving pickup, they'll get there as well – but with different results.

I've seen them get into many forms of trouble. I once watched a group of World War II Polish immigrants, who live in Chicago, as they fished for bass on a farmer's pond. The men were baiting their hand-lines with grasshoppers they caught in the tall grass along the banks and having great success with their easily caught bait.

"Looky here!" one older fellow said in the broken English he learned during his 50 years in America. "With these grasshoppers, I bring them in, one after one! One after one!"

My brother-in-law, Bob, was considered a highly skilled fisherman and watched with wonder as the Polish fellow kept pulling fish from the pond. Meanwhile, Bob and I soaked nearly every bait imaginable, but with no success.

"We'll find something that works," Bob said.

"One after one! One after one!" the Polish fellow boasted.

"Bob, let's try some grasshoppers," I suggested, looking with envy at the Polish guy's catch.

"We'll find something that works," Bob answered.

"One after one! One after one!" the Polish man continued.

Finally, Bob relented and suggested that we catch a couple grasshoppers to see what would happen when we baited our hooks with them.

We caught fish. And then, we caught more fish.

"One after one! One after one!" we finally laughed as we drove away from the pond, our stringers full of bass.

The grasshoppers made for good fishing, but perhaps life wasn't so good for those bold grasshoppers that didn't have the sense to move away from the men.

Grasshoppers become especially bold when you're harvesting the crops they've been using for room and board. One friend complained about how it would startle him when they jumped onto his shirtless back while he was combining oats.

Then, there's the Stickinfinitum. That refers to a grasshopper's ability to hang onto anything, anytime, anywhere. Now, I've seen evidence where that wasn't such a good idea for the bouncy little guys when a combine is involved; they tend to not be so bouncy while they lie among the oats in the bin after having passed through the machinery.

Twenty or 30 of them were clinging to the truck's hood when I drove out of the lane and onto the gravel of Veefkind Road. A rather unscientific experiment showed nary a wiggle from them when the truck was going 25 mph. There was some air-induced movement when I passed 30 mph. But, it wasn't until the speedometer moved past 40 that a few of them started to fall off.

Shucks, it wasn't until after I hit the blacktopped highway and passed 50 mph that they all jumped off, and I believe some jumped on their own accord instead of giving in to the forces of the artificially-induced wind.

Religion teachers told me a few times in catechism classes that all creatures were put on earth to serve a purpose.

So far, the best reason I can find for grasshoppers being here has been for the entertainment of a kid waiting for Dad to make another round with the combine. Then, the kid could look into the oats bin to see grasshoppers trying to jump with a missing rear leg, bounding about at weird angles.

They serve to make people undertake totally unscientific experiments, such as the one I did, to see how long they could hang onto my truck.

And, of course, we can't forget how they make handy fish bait.

New, Old Worries in the Woods

I needed a few minutes to myself the other day, so I headed out to the woods in Veefkind.

There were a few bugs, but not as many as I expected – which made the visit a little more enjoyable than it might have been if that late-August day had been infested with annoying little flying critters.

I had a lot on my mind that day, and I didn't know if the woods were the best place to contemplate things. We'd had a logging operation in the woods $1\frac{1}{2}$ years earlier, and looking at the results was still a little unsettling.

One side of me kept saying that the logging was good for the woodlot. But, the other side of me has always been a little upset with some of the results, such as the deep ruts and treetops left behind.

The woods had been left to look naked in some parts and like a tornado had passed through other parts.

I'd agreed with one of my brothers, John, who once said, "If we were younger again and going to spend as much time hunting squirrels out there as we did as kids, we'd cry if Dad had this done to the woods."

My attempt at finding time for contemplation was to be my first trip into the woods since the previous spring when I had cut some firewood from the downed tree-tops, and piled leftovers in hopes of creating some rabbit and grouse cover.

I was hoping that the re-growth process I'd see during my August visit would make me feel like the work I'd done in the spring had been worthwhile.

A few steps into the woods eased my anguish a little more than I'd expected.

The poplars that had sprouted the summer before were thickening, almost to the point where I was concerned there'd be too much competition among the little trees. Hopefully, I thought, they would thin themselves on their own.

As I scanned one of my favorite sitting-spots, I wished I'd taken more time to do more cutting and piling in the spring. But, even in areas where I hadn't worked, it seemed that the decaying process was well under way, and that nature was doing its job of taking care of the mess the logging had created.

The scene eased my mind more than I'd ever expected. I was noticing an old acorn shell on an oak stump when I remembered all the good times that I had out there as a youngster – just as John had reminded me. The stump was just like one of my favorites that had served as a perch among some oaks; where a young fellow could lay his squirrel rifle across his lap and wait for some squirrel "chattering" to start.

The stump, still fairly fresh from the logging, provided me with the perfect place to sit. There, I could mull over and sort out a lot of things on my mind. I instantly knew it would become one of my favorite spots for years to come.

The stump also helped to ease my mind about what had been done to the woods. While the methods may have been more precise, the stump we sat on as youngsters to hunt squirrels had become a stump because someone back then had logged the woodlot, too.

Time had taken those old stumps, and the trees that had been little more than saplings had matured in the void left by the cut trees. All that remained from those earlier cuttings was an old logging trail, which had started to become grown over because of a lack of use.

The cutting had been done before, and it will be done someday in the future. Someone had fretted about the previous cutting, and someone will fret about a cutting someday in the future. And, every time, the wonder of the woods will ease that person's mind.

We had, through our logging, provided a future for an entirely new generation of trees, and provided another generation of people the chance to experience those wonderful woods.

And, even more important to me at that moment, we'd provided a new stump on which I could leave all my worries.

Splendor in the Northern Sky

The Harvest Moon, which so often comes with a crisp early-fall evening, is a time when most rural people look to the sky with great romance dancing in their eyes.

It's a time that hayrides are on hand; Halloween pranks are just around the corner; when raccoons are abundant in the cornfields.

But, over the years, I think I've found something that brings out my best feelings about life on my land at Veefkind. It dances by itself, seemingly beating your eyes to the feeling that there is something special in the air.

It's the dancing of the Northern Lights about which I write. Aurora Borealis – beams of light emanating from the horizon somewhere in the Far North and shooting far into the fall night sky.

They came out while I drove northward on a recent moonless night. At first, they peeked from the horizon, as though asking whether it was OK for them to appear from their magical hiding place.

Then they appeared, one by one, as though the darkness was a cold swimming hole and the lights were testing the water before each of the child-like fingers of light splashed into the darkness.

I stopped the vehicle on the lonely gravel road that night and turned off the lights in order to drink in all of its show.

I knew I wouldn't receive this show in a town of any size. Street lights of any kind would spoil the event, which can only be appreciated at its fullest with the least possible influence from man-made lighting.

In order to obtain its full brilliance, a sea of stars in a clear sky on a crisp October night can be the only lighting. In their own way, the stars provide special effects lighting far beyond that which could be provided on the most high-tech of light stages.

I watched intently as the Northern Lights became more and more brave, becoming denser by the minute and spreading toward the west, then the east from their points of origin.

That night's show became more spectacular as they spread higher and higher, reaching for the highest of the stars straight above us. Eventually, the fingers reached over our heads and even a bit toward the southern sky, as though challenging their cousins from the south – Aurora Australis – to find a meeting place over my wonderful Veefkind homeland.

The northern sky was fully ablaze with their brightness; their fingers reaching further and further and eventually creating a full band straight above me, running nearly from the western to eastern horizons.

Aurora, they tell me, was the ancient Roman goddess of the dawn, identified by the Greeks with the goddess Eos. Scientifically, they tell me, the lights are caused by the bombardment of the atmosphere with charged solar particles that are being guided along the earth's magnetic lines of force.

The scientific explanation fails to diminish the magnificence of the awe-striking power that the lights emit. I tend to side with the early Greeks and Romans who, like me, stood slack-jawed at the splendor that could only have been created by superior beings within the heavens.

Seldom have I ever witnessed such a display of the lights as on that night in Veefkind. Perhaps I never will again.

But, as with so many of my experiences from that land which for so many generations had provided life, I'll have the memories of that sight to share with others and eventually carry to my grave.

Few who have ever experienced such a show can understand why, for so many of us, the rural countryside has become so important.

No matter how business-like we want – even need – to appear across the rural landscape, for most of us there always will be our own versions of the Northern Lights.

The Woods' Sounds of Silence

Shhhhhhhhhh. Shhhhhhhhhh. Shhhhhhhhhh.

It's the end of the day in the woods. The air had been still throughout the late afternoon; that time when the woods' creatures had been so busy completing their day's chores, has produced three small gusts of breeze that ticked the dried leaves still hanging in the oak trees.

Leaves from the aspen and maples had long since fallen, but the leaves hang onto the oaks long into the winter – some until spring. Day after day, the breeze hitting those oak leaves signals the beginning of the day's end. The animals and the fallen dried leaves from the other trees help pass the signal that night is coming.

Shhhhhhhhhh. Shhhhhhhhhh. Shhhhhhhhhh.

The breeze moves through the oak leaves for one last time. The woods goes silent for five minutes. A damp chill comes with the air, a big change far different than the fall air that moments earlier had been gently warmed by the sun.

Shik chik. Shik chik. Shik chik. Shik chik.

A squirrel breaks the silence as it bounds through the leaves. Maybe the squirrel is checking for one last acorn to bury; maybe it's taking the long route to its nest.

The silence returns, lasting for another minute or two.

Shiiiiiik shiiiiiik shiiiiiik shiiiiiik shiiiiiik shiiiiiik. BBBWOOOWOOOOWOOOWOOO.

A ruffed grouse saunters between the trees, its tail dragging through the leaves, then makes one last thunderous take-off for the day to fly to its favorite roost on a nearby tree's branch.

Again, the silence returns and lasts for about three minutes.

Shik shik shik shik shik shik shik shik shik shik shik shik shik shik shik shik. Chuk chuk chuk chuk chuk chuck chuk!

The squirrel meets another of its kind and a short chase is on, ending with one giving a brief verbal scolding.

More silence, but not for long.

Whufff whufff whufff whufff whufff whufff whufff kerchik kerchik click.

A turkey takes off to reach its perch, the bird's wings – forever too short for its body – fighting, fighting, fighting through the air and then through twigs and small branches to carry its 20 pounds to its night's perch.

About 10 seconds of quiet.

Whufff whufff whufff whufff whufff whufff whufff kerchick kerchick click.

Another 10 seconds of silence.

Whufff whufff whufff whufff whufff whufff whufff kerchick kerchick click.

Another turkey lifts its agile but awkward-looking body to a roost near the first turkey.

Yet another 10 seconds of silence.

Whufff whufff whufff whufff whufff whufff whufff kerchick kerchick click.

Still another turkey takes its turn in finding its way to a perch.

The silence returns. It seems to last this time. All the animals that keep the woods lively during the day are in their nests, holes and roosts.

Quiet finally covers the woods like a quilt pulled up to the chin on a chilly winter night. The quiet amplifies the stillness that had been in the air since those last three bursts of breeze rustled the oak leaves.

The quiet and stillness lasts for nearly a half-hour. Then, as darkness has the woods nearly closed to human sight, comes a sound that serves to remind us that life in those woods exists at all hours.

Shhhuk chuk shhhuk chuk shhhuk chuk shhhuk chuk. Whoooh! Chump chump. Chump chump. Chump chump. Chump chump.

It's a deer moving along to make its night-rounds, maybe stopping for a moment to crunch an acorn with its teeth; maybe just passing through on its way to feed in a nearby hay field. It senses danger and gives a whistling blow to signal other deer of the danger, then escapes in four large bounds.

Eventually, the silence will be broken by another breeze or by more of the woods' night animals. There will be more long moments of silence as the night continues.

But there is only that one time, which some call the witching hour, when the sounds and feel of the air say it's time for the day to end; the signal for the woods and its creatures to rest and prepare for another new day.

The Call of the Geese

Sleep was about to overtake me when barking in the distance gained my attention. I hoped for a moment that if it was a distant neighbor's dog, whatever was making the animal bark soon would disappear, or the dog would become bored and stop barking.

More barking. More barking. More barking.

It was no longer the sound of a single animal barking. It was two. It was three. It was four.

Even more barking, and it was coming closer, each minute becoming easier to hear through the open bedroom window on such a warm fall night.

The near-sleep numbness left my mind and my senses sharpened; I realized it was one of those special sounds of fall. It was a night movement of a flock of Canada geese.

Sigurd Olson was one of my favorite writers. He spent many years in the wilderness along the border between Minnesota and Canada. When not canoeing or reminiscing about his surroundings, he was waxing poetic about the sounds of loons.

Loons, to a great extent, became a Sigurd Olson trademark.

It's easy to understand what made Olson feel and write about loons as he did. Anyone who has ever fallen under the spell of loons' calls can understand his obsession with the little understood lake birds.

In great part because of Olson's musings, loons and their calls have become trademarks of the Northwoods' lake country.

Bald eagles, once such rare sights anywhere but places like Alaska, have made a comeback in my part of the world. The pride they exude as they soar or sit high in a tree along a river's edge brings hushed ooos and aaaahs from anyone. Hearing an eagle's scream quiets the ooos and aaaahs and results in slack-jawed looks of awe.

Loons and eagles have earned their place in Northwoods' lore. But I'd like to make the case for geese.

Geese rival any creature in signaling spring or fall. Their honking sparks expectation. Those who hope to hear their honking are people who know the feel of heart-quickening anticipation.

So often, their sound has come to me just as it did on that quiet night as I was about to sleep. It starts with that single, distant barking sound. More often than not, I've wondered whether the sound actually was a dog barking in the distance.

As they near, the sound becomes that of two or three dogs barking sporadically. Then it becomes the sound of a group of playing children. Then it grows into the sound of a playground full of children; then to the overwhelming sound of a playground full of children yelling as a pack of dogs barks at them.

Many of my favorite moments have been spent in a goose blind or hidden in standing corn along the edge of a cornfield that already had been harvested. Those are times when a warm cup of coffee can be shared with a hunting partner; even some quiet chatter about what worldly – or for that matter unworldly – events are going on in our lives.

In our goose hunting world, there is little need for keeping a keen eye on the sky. Any exposure of even the white of an eye would alert geese to our presence – they can see something as slight as an eye movement far sooner than a human eye can see distant geese flying. A goose that spots a hunter quickly climbs to heights far outdistancing a shotgun's range or simply changes direction to avoid the hunter.

Whispers of conversation with a hunting partner and sips of coffee help stave off the bite in the fall air and sometimes a freezing drizzle or even snow.

The stiff muscles and joints that form while hiding in those cold places go unnoticed with the magic of hearing that first distant barking sound made by a goose. Breathing deepens and heartbeats quicken with the anticipated growth of the flock's noise, and increases as the geese near.

The noise of the geese as they get nearer, that sound like children playing and dogs barking, is overwhelming.

If homework and preparation has been done well enough, the geese might start to land within a few yards and sometimes even within a few feet of hiding hunters.

Being in the middle of 50, 100 or even 200 landing geese is like being put into a wind tunnel with thousands of $100 bills being blown around.

Which to grab? Spin. Look. Try to choose.

Those who haven't experienced being within that landing circle – even those who have but aren't mentally prepared – can quickly become disoriented.

The disorienting effects of a flock of geese isn't always the result of being caught in the middle of a landing.

Another of my favorite times to hear geese involves becoming disoriented with them while they soar hundreds of yards overhead while I cross a farmyard or relax in the woods on those spring or fall migration days. Those times don't come with the confusion of being in the middle of the landing, but I can get lost in the romance and freedom of their flight. The adventure and the beauty of our country that the geese will see is the envy of people who don't like to spend their lives within walls.

The geese seem to own the clean, crisp air that they breathe and which lifts them.

The routes the geese travel are full of challenges. But I'm sure being able to soar high and free as the geese do makes it worthwhile to face those challenges.

A smile crossed my lips as I listened to the geese pass overhead as I lay in bed that night, picturing in my mind the low-flying flock picking out small towns' street lights and rural yard lights to direct them in their travels.

I slipped into sleep as the last of that flock's sounds disappeared into the dark country air. My lasting memory of that night was realizing the excitement and comforts I've felt over the years.

The geese again had competed well with the loons and eagles.

Leaves in the Woods

The brisk fall air pierced my lungs as I climbed out of my truck for a walk in my wonderful woods at Veefkind the other morning.

It was the type of morning for which I'd longed for many days. The sunrise had, moments before, brought a bright, orange hue to the eastern horizon; the sky above opening itself to accept the deep blue the morning sunlight would offer.

Only days had passed since I last visited the place where I've spent so much of my time – the place that provides such a recharging effect to my inner being.

Accepting that it had been only days since I'd visited was difficult on this day, though. When I'd last been there at the same time of the morning, the sunrise had reflected bright reds, yellows, golds, browns and greens from the fall leaves that hung from the maple, aspen and oak trees dominating the woods.

This day, only the growing blue of the morning sky came through the treetops. The leaves had signaled the nearing winter by falling to the small forest's floor. There, they would provide a blanket of protection from the two or three feet of snow that soon would try to frostbite the toe-like roots that crawl many generations deep into the life-giving duff.

The freezer-like cold of that morning air, and the lack of leaves rustling from the trees brought a freshness to the woods – a freshness that jolted my senses almost like having jumped into a tub of ice-water after having taken a long run on a hot July morning. The freshness came with a silence that almost allowed me to hear my own heartbeat.

I tried to be quiet as I entered the trail which, so often in early fall, had carried me to the special stump I love to sit upon to drink in the sights and sounds of that place deep in the heart of Wisconsin.

But, the quietness was unforgiving. With every step, loud crunches echoed from beneath my feet, announcing my approach to any creatures that may view me as nothing less than trouble.

I looked down to see what looked like trillions of leaves there on the ground; the brightness of their beauty having

Rural Routes & Ruts

left, just as the ducks and geese that had so beautifully swam on the nearby ponds had left for the year.

I picked up one of the leaves and pondered its life, feeling the paper-like skin that had soaked in the sun's summer warmth. I felt along its veins, through which the sun and moisture had pumped life and added strength into one of the trees. I felt its stem and sensed the firmness of the grip it had used to hold its mother-tree throughout strong spring and summer winds and storms.

The leaf, only a few months ago, had shown itself as a bud on the end of one of the tree's limbs. It had emerged like a butterfly leaving its cocoon, soon spreading itself to dry in the spring air.

The leaf would appear to be solitary if I focused on its new life on that limb. But, there was much more to its world than its singular existence, I knew.

The years of observing the lives of similar leaves on the trees at Veefkind reminded me to draw back from the single leaf. Doing that allows me to see its many siblings on nearby limbs. It allows me to see the strong but gentle way in which the strongest of oaks hold their leaves, much like my Midwestern parents had held me.

Drawing back even more, I often had seen many such families exist on many trees, making me realize how, like us, the trees formed their own communities. And, within those communities, I could see diversity exploding with the varied species of trees and plants coexisting there.

They not only coexist well with their own plant "world." Indeed, they invite all forms of life to exist with them, the squirrels and deer and rabbits and birds and so many other creatures that enter – me included.

The leaf was cold and lifeless in my hand, the frost which covered it with white melting a numbing wetness onto my fingers.

I gently crumbled it into the palm of my hand, my fingers forming a fist engulfing its entirety.

I longed for the ability to provide any of the wonders such as those it had offered me throughout its life.

I longed for its ability to serve so much without question.

But, then human arrogance told me that, even with all of the beauty the leaf had provided me, I had an advantage.

Unlike that leaf, I was able to contemplate its life – and, conversely, my life.

As I grew older, I realized, I would be able to understand more about what makes me enjoy that Veefkind woods and the generations of leaves and people that had been there before me.

That's a good thing to know on a cold November morning.

The Land's Love isn't Jealous

The snow was smooth, the cold still air having left nary a ripple across its white elegance.

It needed tracks. It needed form. It was as though the snow called to be walked upon.

I looked at the pristine snow that covered the wetland grasses between the woodlots out at Veefkind. It was easy to see the need for tracks to give the snow form and add life to the scene.

The snow and the land, I believed, like a jealous love, once again were using their alluring beauty to call me.

The Veefkind woods is like that. It's always been possessive of me. It's where I grew up, where I learned so much about life.

It wasn't long before we were on snowshoes and crossing the marsh. I broke the virgin snow's surface with my long snowshoes and Pam, the mother of my children, followed on a shorter pair. The combination of the still-fluffy snow and the tall grass it covered made for a good challenge.

A few beads of sweat were forming on my brow when my attention was drawn to a wildlife pond which, true to the day's form, also beckoned for tracks to be made across its snowy surface.

Pam warned me as I answered the pond's call. Perhaps the heavy snow cover hadn't allowed the pond to fully freeze, even though the winter temperature had many times already slipped below zero.

But, the pond seemed to call me forth. I confidently stepped across its frozen surface until I reached the very middle. There, I stopped to turn and inform Pam that, just this time, maybe her intuition had been misdirected.

Heavy, wet slush suddenly began to cover my snowshoes as I so boldly spoke. The slush started to suck my snowshoes and boots into the pond's water. As I struggled, the quicksand-like snowy water only took my feet deeper into the pond.

After a determined fight, I worked my way back to the edge of the pond, the snowshoes bearing the weight of some of the freezing slop that had tried to take my pack boots to the pond's muddy bottom.

I laughed at my foolishness as I reached the pond's edge. There would have been no real danger; the pond's greatest depth may not have reached above my thighs.

I was even willing to listen to a chorus of "I told you so."

The afternoon of snowshoeing continued across the open marsh and into the woodlots, as we worked hard to leave our temporary imprint on the land that has given so much to us.

I drove past the land a few days later as I passed through Veefkind. I stopped to reflect at the tracks we'd made; reminding myself how, like those tracks – which had been blown full with snow – we were only temporary. They were temporary just as the cold of winter eventually yields to the warm spring sun.

That's when I realized that the Veefkind woods is a jealous place. Like a jealous lover, it calls often and with growing intensity.

The land uses the lure of the romance of so many childhood memories it has left in my heart; of the freshness of crisp winter days, the newness of spring, the heat of summer and the sights and smells of fall afternoons.

It calls me as a place of romance, with the excitement of new and wonderful experiences each time I view its beauty.

As I reflected upon making the first tracks in that snow and the pond wanting to pull my feet to its muddy bottom, I realized that this is a love from which I'll never escape.

I have traveled to the opposite side of the globe. But, no matter where I travel, part of my heart always will be in that central Wisconsin place I call Veefkind. But, I realized it wasn't the land acting like a jealous love that lured me back; it was the fact that it could let me move forward which made me keep a special place for it in my heart.

I'd felt the need to escape as soon as the slush pulled me toward the pond's bottom. I knew it's the same with people – as soon as we jealously try to pull someone too close, there will be an urge to resist.

Jealousy is a terrible thing, which strangles love to death.

The Veefkind land has, without jealousy, given me good reminders of how much I still belong to its soil. And, my heart will continue to respond to its call, returning again to make tracks across the fresh snow.

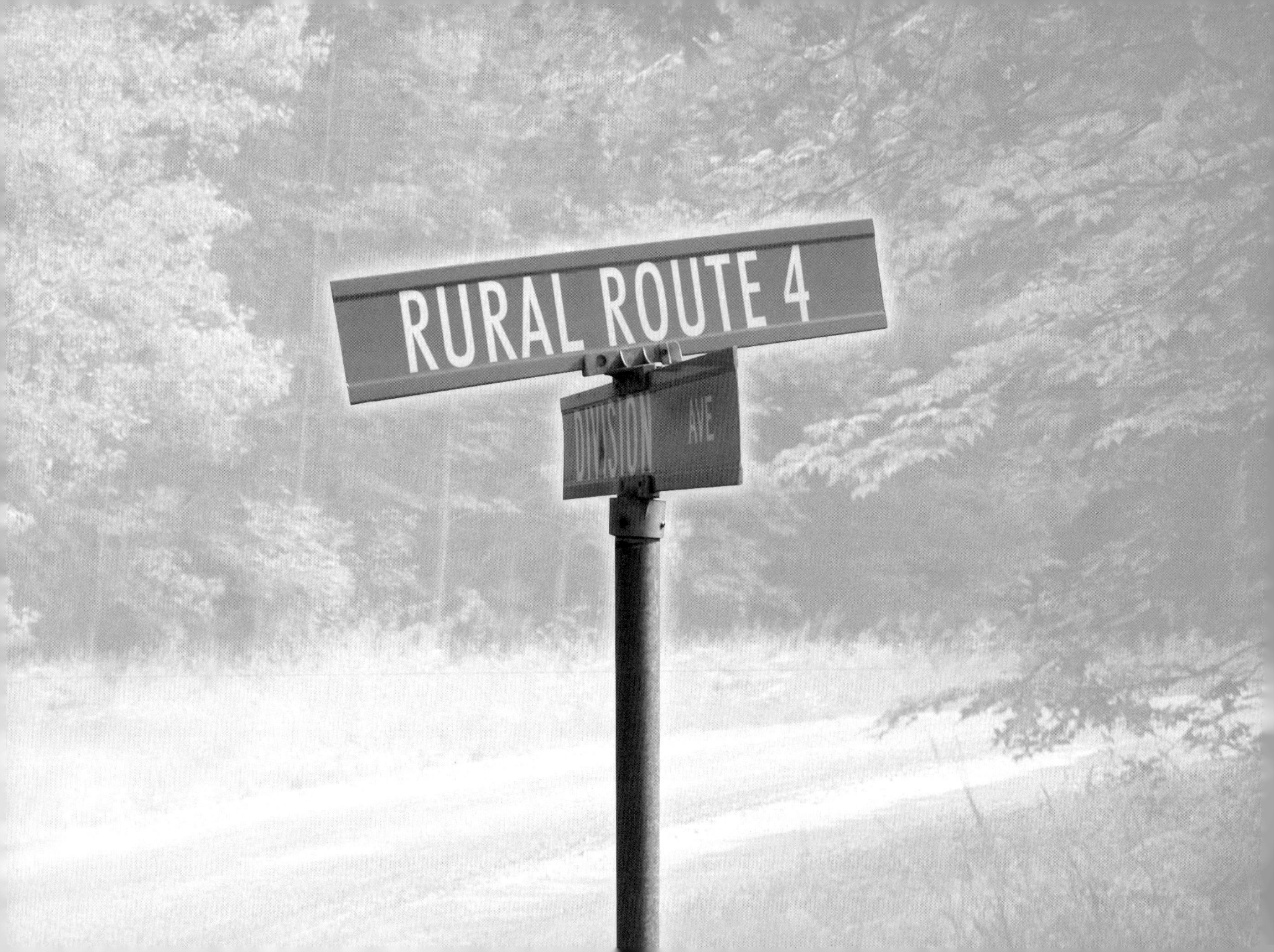
RURAL ROUTE 4
DIVISION AVE

Rural Necessities

The Good of Being Born in a Barn

In my world, it's common to hear the insult, "Were you born in a barn?"

Leave a door open and Mother said it.

If I walked into school with mud on my feet, the teacher said it.

Trying to eat my peas with my table knife would have my sisters saying it.

"Born in a barn." I used to think it was the ultimate insult.

Nobody wanted to be known for having been born in a barn. In fact, I can think of only one family that's openly admitted their son was born in a barn and, considering who that person is, I'm certain few people ever chastised him for it – at least I think that wasn't a primary cause for him having been nailed to a cross.

"Born in a barn." I've given that a lot of thought in recent years and have come to the conclusion that, yes, I really may have been "born" in a barn.

No, my parents hadn't needed to deal with the inconveniences of enduring my physical birth within the walls of a barn. The "birth" to which I refer is my spiritual birth – the "birth" of who I really am.

That version of my birth started with me watching with wide eyes as my parents and five older siblings made their way through the daily chores in our family's old dairy barn. The barn pulsed with the lives of our Holstein cows, some calves, a few cats and our dog.

I grew to be able to complete small chores, at a very young age carrying small pails of milk and feeding the calves. But at such a young age, I often lay on bags of grain stacked in the barn, dreaming of days when I could be among those older people who were able to do the farm's "real" work.

The days of "real" work came all too quickly, it seemed, and wasn't nearly as glorious as I'd imagined. Though, looking back, I can see that work's character-building qualities.

Even as I begrudgingly grew into being responsible for more of the work, I spent increasing amounts of time with siblings and neighborhood friends in that barn – the one my great-great-grandfather had built in the mid-1800s.

There were races to be held in the barn alley during winter Saturday afternoons; there was basketball to be played; there were forts to be built, and new litters of kittens to be found within the bales when the haymow was full.

Visions of fantastic athletic fetes floated in the haymow. Fingers were numbed by the cold late-winter night air while dribbling a basketball on the uneven haymow floor-boards, the ball having become under-inflated in the cold air. I could be John McGlockin of the Milwaukee Bucks, throwing up 20 footers as I listened to Eddie Doucette's calls over the blaring barn radio: "Johnny 'Mac' from the corner… bango!" Or I'd be Kareem "on the skyhook" or Bobby "The Rabbit" Dandridge working in the "toaster" or "The Big O" shooting his one-handed free throws.

On any given day, I might be Russ Hellickson or Dan Gable, doing pull-ups on pipes or challenging myself to see how many bags of barn lime I could carry, with hopes of Olympic wrestling glory still part of my dreams.

The barn allowed me to be Rocky Balboa before his time.

It wasn't until later in life that I realized how the jumping and the bouncing ball created intensely loud thumping and dust that fell onto milking equipment, the main reasons for Dad's admonitions for me to stop playing and to get working.

On a given Saturday afternoon, the barn could be a place of solitude and reflection, or a place where large calves found themselves transformed into bucking rodeo animals.

No harm ever came to the animals during those impromptu "rodeos." The only concerns about well-being was ours, after our parents discovered that we'd been using the calves for bucking bronc and bull-riding events.

It's likely that I spent more time in that barn working, playing and even contemplating life during my first 18 years of life than I had spent in our family's house.

Sometimes, I wish I hadn't left it. But I did, and can't go back, except for brief moments to touch the barn's weathered boards or to inhale the alluring aromas of its haymow.

Though I can never fully go back, I can take pleasure in knowing and remembering the things I learned and did in that barn. It's the place where I've laughed, cried, worked, played, hid, thought and all else that goes with being a young man.

I was born there. As with the genetics passed to me by my ancestors, the barn has instilled in me its own form of genetics and played a large role in making me who I am – whether it's the good or the bad.

I know now that having someone ask me whether I was born in a barn can't be considered an insult.

Ask me today whether I was born in a barn and my chest is likely to swell with pride before I respond with a resounding "Yes!"

Important Farm Tools

Some tools around the farm are a little more valuable than others; value isn't necessarily determined by the tool's price.

That came to mind as I eyed the workbench one day at the home farm in Veefkind. I wasn't certain, but I believe one of the hammers there may actually have belonged to me. I brought it to the attention of my brother, who lived at the farm, and he agreed it might be – and it reminded him how I might have his cross-cut saw.

As I drove out of the farm's yard, claw hammer lying on my truck's floorboard, I thought about how it's the borrowing of small tools that can get you bounced out of a farm yard faster than you can say "jackknife."

The "perfect family" suburban television shows of the late 1950s and the early 1960s (the ones where Mom wears 4-inch heels and pearls, and Dad wears a tie to the dinner table every night) once had me believe that borrowing feuds actually had something to do with tools like lawn mowers and power drills.

Go ahead and borrow tools like those in places like Veefkind. Heck, borrow the guy's tractor or plow or wagons or anything of high value. They know where to find you and their high-priced equipment.

But, if you want to know where you really stand, you have to lie under a piece of equipment and help the same guy fix something in the field and, in the process, borrow his *important* tools.

"Lemme see your pliers so I can spread this cotter pin and then we can get back to work," you might say.

"Make sure I get it back," the guy will reflexively say as he plucks his pliers from a well-worn holder hanging from his belt.

"Dang, there's some baler-twine wrapped around this shaft; gimme your jackknife so I can cut it off, then you can get back to your business," you might add a few minutes later.

"Forget to give it back to me, and you might find yourself wrapped around that shaft," he's likely to say, as he reluctantly hands over his prized knife.

I've been around guys who'd as soon not get the equipment fixed, than hand over something as important as their pliers or jackknife.

It's those little tools, I've decided, which really make the world run. People say we're coming to a point where quick-information computer systems are vital to our every

Rural Routes & Ruts

move, but those systems aren't going anywhere without the "little tools" needed for maintenance and repairs.

I've seen entire baling operations shut down for lack of a jackknife needed to cut the excess twine from the ends of a well-tied square knot, between old and new balls of twine.

I think a lot of value farmers hold for pliers and jackknives has something to do with the tools' usefulness. I've seen them used for everything from wrench, to hammer, to screwdriver, to castrating knife, to apple slicer. The only hope I ever have for the tools is that they are wiped clean between the jobs, especially of castrating piglets and slicing apples.

I felt a twinge of guilt as I drove out of my brother's yard with the hammer in my truck, because I wasn't positive it was one of my long-lost hammers. It might have been one that only looked like my hammer. I thought about how I'd eventually call my brother and tell him, but remind him how we weren't sure the hand saw he hauled from my garage last spring actually was his, either.

I also might have asked him if he still had one of those jackknives the old dairy plant presented to its patrons about 25 years earlier. It would be strange if he didn't have one and I did; he was one of the plant's patrons and I wasn't.

Maybe that dairy-plant gift "fell" into my pocket one of those days when I was helping my brother bale hay. I know I wouldn't have removed it from his possession on purpose – he's much bigger than me.

With the value placed on tools like that knife, I decided it might have been best to develop a way for him to "find" it somewhere else – a place where he might have "lost' it in years past.

Cutting Through the Myths of Work

My intensity grew with each swing of the dulled ax.

Cracking. Slamming. Smashing. Splintering. Breaking.

Through the intensity, I didn't notice that a piece of wood had splintered from the windfall tree that I was hacking on to use later as firewood; the piece that put a small cut into the muscle on the outside of my right shin.

It was work that could have been done in a few moments with a chainsaw. Unfortunately – or fortunately, as I take a more romantic view – the nearest chainsaw was a couple hours' drive from the cabin I'd found in the depth of a woods.

My muscles flexed from deep within as I swung the ax again and again. Its pointed edge, though dull, seemed to hunger for every bite it could make into the wood.

As the ax hungered, my body hungered for more. More sweat. More exertion. More pain, the sort of pain that actually brings about a good feeling.

"How had I allowed myself to miss the beauty of this sort of physical labor?" I wondered.

I know down deep that such labor, when done as a daily requirement, wouldn't have much of that joy I was feeling each time the ax went over my head to prepare for slamming down into the seemingly defenseless wood. Still, I regretted missing opportunities to do more of what I've always thought of as honest labor – the sort in which a man's body feels his labors at the end of the day.

If I was to vow to do more of that honest labor, how long would I keep that vow? How long before my editor's chair beckoned to again make me feel the false sensation of "work" while laboring within the walls of an office?

The reality was that I would soon be returning to my rural town – inhabited by some who know of honest physical labor and some who don't. There, I might return to my running regimen to try replicating the exercise I'd get through physical labor. But there, the swings of the ax in that woods soon would become only a memory.

I'll forever cherish what I'd gained through having been raised to know the greatness of lifting, sweating, pushing, pulling, groaning and hurting in a daily work routine.

But those days of honest, physical work are past for me. Seldom will I feel the energy pouring from my aging body – and the release of many of my frustrations – as I felt during those couple of hours I spent with that ax in the woods.

A Farm's Fossils

The newspaper photograph showed a man holding a rock outlined with a fossil thousands of years old.

We don't hear too much about those kinds of finds where I come from. It's always seemed that the soil of my Veefkind home somehow hadn't been there prior to the mid-1800s settlement of European immigrants; certainly not much earlier than the early occasional visits by Native Americans. Around Veefkind, we hear only of an occasional find of a Native American tool and only once have I heard of such a find that was more than 5,000 years old.

We don't find dinosaur bones in Veefkind. We don't find pottery. We don't find 10,000-year-old human remains, preserved or unpreserved. Those finds seem to be the property of more exotic locations on other continents.

I'm not an archeologist, so I don't know why we don't have the massive digs for fossils we see in other parts of the world. Maybe the Ice Age took care of all that for us, having long scraped any worthwhile artifacts somewhere to the south of here.

But I do know future archeologists will have plenty to look at around Rural Route Veefkind.

These archeological thoughts came to mind one day while I was walking through an area grown over with waist-high grass.

The area had once been part of a busy farmyard. But as with so many small farms of the era, the pulse of this place had stopped at least 20 years before my walk. It had gone quietly, I remember, the victim of a simple sale to neighbors who'd been expanding their farm.

There hadn't been a struggle over the farm's existence. Its former owners were old and its new owners – likely even more adept in the ways of conservation and sustainability than the old owners – made for a cordial and sensible transaction.

Prior to their departure, the old owners had parked plenty of machinery around the farmyard. Some machinery, its functional days long past, had been parked there many years before the farm's sale.

I knew some of the machinery in that overgrown grass had been used two – some maybe even three – generations before me. There were pieces there with which I was unfamiliar. I'd have needed an old farmer's explanation of its workings, I knew, had the grass been willing to release its powerful, twisted and tangled hold on the machinery.

There's plenty about that era of machinery of which I knew little, even though I may have seen Grandpa working with some of it at one time or another.

That farm, I knew, wasn't alone in serving as a mausoleum for such machinery. There were farms across the countryside, where the grip of similar grass was pulling machinery into the very earth on which a farmer had earlier so proudly used those implements.

Old machinery is parked in orchards, around old building foundations, and countless brushy or wooded rural back 40s.

It's there for eternity. Maybe it would stay above the ground, safely covered in the brush and grass. Or, it might eventually meet the blade of a bulldozer, to be buried under the weight of its beloved soil, then to feel the weight of another generation of progress pressing it farther from the surface.

In the weeds, I found a wheel that once had been rimmed with rubber. But many years of exposure to the sun, rain, heat, cold and wind had decayed the tire from the rim it had protected. Any trace of the rubber would have to be sifted from the dirt around the wheel.

Beside the wheel lay the rusted beam from a frame.

That was all there was to it, that frame and that wheel. It seemed to be up to me to guess from what the parts might have been.

Perhaps they were parts of a trailer; maybe a wagon that had hauled loads of loose hay behind the power of a first-generation McCormik-Deering tractor or a team of faithful horses.

I wondered for a while what was going on when the mysterious implement was fresh from a factory. Had the Doughboys returned from their expeditions against Kaiser Wilhelm's Germany? Was it leaned on by farmers who were discussing the tough economic times of the Great Depression?

Maybe it hadn't even been built in a factory at all. Maybe a handy and creative young farmer had built it from spare parts of old machines from still another previous generation.

Old equipment was important to my old neighbor, a man who spent endless hours building, creating, and fixing. Some of the machinery resembled its original form; some became parts of new equipment. Aging equipment in the weeds seemed to give him life.

But, there weren't many answers about the decaying wagon – or whatever else the parts were from. I also lacked answers about the remains of an old four-wheeled manure spreader I found in another spot that day.

Someday, however, there will be even more questions about the machinery than the questions I could have had. Someday, perhaps an archeologist's shovel may bump into one of the parts, and the treasure hunter will be even more excited about the discovery than I could have been.

Someday, stories will be told about the gems, which for a generation many years earlier, had been used and then discarded as junk. They'll tell about farmers who used a shovel to clean manure from their barns' gutters, and who didn't think twice about the magic sound of steel horse-drawn equipment jingling across the fields.

Someday, a man may have his photograph taken as he holds a rock containing the imprint of a wheel – a wheel which long before had become part of the earth's duff.

That man probably will be amazed and maybe amused at the primitive farming practices used in the first half of the 20th century.

Hopefully, that man can have the same earthly sense and values held by people who'd used that ancient piece of farm equipment.

Hopefully, there will be humans be left on Earth to make such discoveries.

Hopefully, humans will have learned from the triumphs and mistakes made by generations that had known that machinery's use.

Places to Hide

Everybody should have their corners of the world where they can go for solitude; that place that no more than one or two very close friends know about. It has to be a place of self-contemplation or where those ever-so-special friends can go with you to whisper about all that's important in life.

A handful of such places existed for a couple of kids who grew up in that rural place called Veefkind.

Maybe other people knew about them, but just allowed those boys to think the spots really were special hiding places. Since the boys grew up and had children of their own, it was easy to understand that parents have a special sense of knowing where the places are, but it's best to let the boys keep thinking those places are special.

One Veefkind boy found the heights of a silver maple tree as one of his sanctuaries. He'd occasionally scale the tree to lie across one of the larger, high limbs to soak in the sun creeping through the leaves. It had a good view of the entire farm, and the rustling of the leaves helped shut out the distracting noises.

Unfortunately, some of the shut out noises were his parents' calls as they sought their son's services for farm chores – at least he'd unwisely told them he couldn't hear their calls until after he'd climbed from the tree. A mother weary from her day's chores and a father short on patience saw little humor in the "I really couldn't hear you" explanation.

Besides, only the youngster could see any sort of safety in the heights of a tree.

Come to think of it, there probably could be little real safety – especially by today's age of rubberized playgrounds and eagle-eyed soccer moms – in most of the places where the kids of Veefkind found their sanctuary.

We were the champions of fort-building within the neighborhood barns. There were tunnels. There were secret chambers. The fact that cats chose the tunnels and forts as safe places to birth their kittens should be enough to show why young boys could find their personal safety there.

Tunnels and chambers built in the depths of hay bales are the ultimate sound-absorbing chambers. They are warmth. Mazes of tunnels made with bales are protection from all enemies – older brothers and sisters, neighborhood stray dogs, interplanetary invaders, and whatever foreign forces our ancestors may have met in wars.

Refuge also could be found beneath the earth. As I think more about it, those hiding places weren't beneath the earth as much as just under a few layers of gravel. The young boys of Veefkind often could be found in culverts – one in particular known as … well, "The Culvert."

Rural Routes & Ruts

The Culvert was large enough for pre-teen boys to get through with a crouch and quite easily by crawling. There, plans for the rest of the day, the rest of the week, the rest of the month, the rest of the year – sometimes even the rest of our lives – were discussed.

The Culvert's concrete wall held out the elements and the many things the bale forts held out. More important, its wall kept inside the ever-so-secret conversations that 11-year-olds can have.

Ken, my neighbor and friend, and I spent hours in that culvert at great risk, we thought. His siblings had convinced us how a car driving over the culvert would cause our eardrums to break – and, through adult life, we've laughed at our gullibility.

In more creative times, the place of safety could be in a lean-to crafted from small trees along the railroad spur line running through the area.

There, boys could share their Huck Finn-like dreams. A squirrel might as well have been a mountain lion; a blue jay might as well have been an eagle.

The Culvert. Hay forts. Trees. Lean-tos. They serve well as safe places for farm boys who have so much to do; so much to think about; so much to talk about with friends.

Maybe the boys from town had their own places of safety. I couldn't guess where they might be. I hope for their sake that they did, for the dreams, goals and ideas that come from those safe places helped shape many rural boys like those from Veefkind.

A Little Church's Story in Me

Journalists are taught early in their careers to not become too close to a story – to report the story without becoming part of it.

That thought flashed through my mind as I saw my brother-in-law balancing a cup of coffee in one hand, and pulling the rope of the church-bell tolling the church's final mass. I greeted him and found a pew, where moments later I would listen to a bishop declare St. Stephen's Catholic Church closed, after 100 years of religious celebration.

This story would be compelling enough for any caring reporter, I thought, even if it was the first time he had stepped foot into the church. It was easy to sense the sadness and the loss in the eyes and voices of the parishioners, many of whom had spent a lifetime of Sundays worshipping there.

That loss and sadness weighed heavy on my heart, too. Maybe it was too heavy a weight for the job I was there to complete.

But there was too much emotion for me to not allow this story to push at my feelings. The altar from which the bishop and the church's last two priests said the final mass meant too much for me to feel objectivity.

The last time I'd been in the church was early October 1996. My mother's casket was in front of that altar, and hers was the last funeral in the church.

I'd watched my father receive his first communion as a member of the Catholic community a few years earlier. I'd held my Godson as he was baptized there.

Three of my five brothers and sisters stood before that altar and exchanged marriage vows.

I'd rung the small bell in the doorway between the altar and sanctuary on many Wednesday nights, Saturday nights and Sunday mornings, announcing the priest's entrance at the beginning of masses. The altar steps on which the bishop stood, before making the closing declaration, served as kneelers for me when I acted as an altar boy.

I glanced around the church's 22 pews and saw many of the same faces I'd seen many years ago during Saturday morning and Wednesday night religious education classes. With them were the faces of many of the people who'd volunteered time to drive some sort of morals into our developing minds – which were often too preoccupied with other teenage matters to allow concentration on the religious lessons those volunteers so faithfully offered.

Many of those former religion teachers seemed to have aged quite well, I thought, considering the torment we sometimes put them through as they tried to help us understand those important lessons.

There were display tables full of scrapbooks and photos of the church's history. I looked at a yellowed page with a summer Bible school photo, and recalled the Rosandiches, the Rands, the Wolfs, the Whites, the Welches, the Steiners, the Zaleskis, the Klimmers – and so many others with whom I'd spent recesses honing my tackling skills in games sometimes too rough for our own good.

The church was full of relatives on the day of its final mass. Many were blood relatives; I saw Dad fight the lump forming in his throat during the final hymn. My Uncle Lawrence and Aunt Helen were selected to make the final communion offering. Nieces sang solos and played the organ and piano; brothers and sisters sang in the choir.

I realized virtually everyone in the church had become related to me in some form over the years. We were the family of St. Stephen's Catholic Church, and I firmly believe there are family bonds that were formed in that church – bonds that go beyond the normal definition of "family."

I once thought it would be better for me to attend the same church as all of my school friends. Children from at

Roaming the Roads of Rural Life

least six school districts gathered for worship and education several times a week at St. Stephen's, but very few were from my school. I realized during the closing mass how lucky I was to have become friends with so many children from those other schools.

The church, to a youngster's eyes, seemed like a big place. But it seemed small as the bishop recited his final words, and grew smaller as the St. Stephen's Choir sang its final hymn.

Aunt Helen would later describe the loss of our church as a funeral without a casket. Her words pounded into my chest; my chest which, as the bishop and priests cleared the church's altar, had tightened just as it had during my mother's funeral.

I blinked away tears and drew a deep breath and sighed.

"Don't become part of this story," I told myself, as friends and relatives filed out of the church for a final time.

No, I wouldn't become part of the story. The story was already part of me.

The Land vs. the Sprawl Beast

Sometimes, the world becomes too loud and we feel the need to get to a quiet spot.

Sometimes, there isn't a quiet spot to be found because the Sprawl Beast is so near. Then, our minds must be able to take us to our special, quiet places.

I noticed how loud things were one day as I visited a farm on the edge of a midwestern college town. That town is small by metropolitan standards with fewer than 30,000 people. But by the standards of many rural folks, it's a town somewhat substantial in its size.

Even a town of that size has been working hard at encroaching into the hills and valleys surrounding it. The farm I visited was nestled between some hills on the edge of the town, just a good stone's throw from the Mississippi River.

Once at the farm, it was hard to believe the homes valued in the many hundreds of thousands of dollars being built along its edges. It's hard to believe the difference in the pace of things outside of the farm's fences. On the outside, we dodged cars zipping through confusing intersections. On the inside, we stopped during our walk to allow some farm geese to cross our path.

The farm's borders will forever be kept sacred by a conservation easement, but the stench of gluttonous

Sprawl Beast's breath overpowers the odors from the farm animals' manure.

That Sprawl Beast has tried to open its mouth to devour the farm. Though the conservation easement is the legal document that will hold the farm's land sacred, the surrounding hills seem to be keeping the beast at bay.

Still, it's difficult for the hills or even the conservation rules to keep the beast silent. It growls throughout the day and night, making the sounds that so often go with development. There is the steady sound of traffic breaking through the farm's trees, seeming to disguise itself as strong gusts of wind. Sirens pierce the crispness of a moonless, star-filled late November sky. Trains rumbling in the distance make us believe that the beast has eaten and digested yet another piece of pristine land.

This farm, and so many like it, had the ultimate answer to the beast's presence. As long as the Sprawl Beast can be kept at a distance, the land will care for us and remind us of what was, of what should be.

A stroll down a path along one of the spring-fed creeks that cross through the farm pulled us into the valley's rich loam, covering us with a blanket that shielded us from the piercing morning wind and warmed us. It bathed us with the calming gurgling of the creek. It got us wonderfully lost in the trees and brush along the creekbeds.

Before we realized it, the Sprawl Beast had been scrubbed from our minds in a way that only the farm's dirt, streams and woodlands can scrub. We couldn't see the beast. We couldn't smell the beast. And best of all, we couldn't hear the beast.

I'm sure the beast's sounds were still present. But when a man allows himself to feel the depth of the land – when he allows himself to be absorbed into the land – it's easy to shut out the presence of the Sprawl Beast – or, for that matter, the presence of any other concerns that can be so distracting.

It's a bit troubling when we know that's a requirement; so many of us preferring days when we wouldn't have to depend so much on the security of our beloved land to save us from the sights, sounds and smells of sprawl. We long for a time when there wasn't such a need. We long for a time when our concerns were simpler and we were able to give our attention to the land, instead of hoping the land would give its attention to us.

I appreciate the land for the way it provides a refuge; how it provides a quiet place when there seems there can be no way to find quiet.

I hope to find ways to return the favor to the land – to its soil, its streams, its brush and its trees.

Time for returning the favor is short, but I don't think it's too late. At least I hope there's time, because the world is getting pretty loud and I need a quiet place.

Rural Routes & Ruts

Painting the Face of Rural Life

We writers so often pride ourselves in waxing poetic about the wonders of our favorite places, especially those of us who fancy ourselves knowledgeable about that wonderful landscape we know as rural America.

The open sky. The comfort of rustling leaves in a woodlot. The calls of meadowlarks and loons. The popping of a good campfire. The smell of fresh-cut clover and alfalfa. The chilling dampness of dew on our feet while chasing cows on an early June morning. The sight of a fox or a fisher slinking across an open field. The joys of playing hide-and-seek in a field of tall corn. The sound of a plow opening sod.

Writers join other artists in sharing all we know about our beloved rural land; those who use photographs, songs and paintings to express what we work to pull from our hearts in the form of words.

Sometimes I wonder whether we're doing our jobs too well.

Evidence of my suspicions can be found across the countryside, in the form of housing complexes popping up in one farm field after another. People apparently are seeing the beauty we have for so many years shared through our art — and they want to be part of that beauty.

What we so willingly share, we often so jealously guard.

Our discomfort grows as those who want to be more a part of our rural world shoulder their way into the countryside. The housing developments expand. The highways grow. Divisions between town and country become blurred.

Those who shared everything good about the rural land and its people find themselves asking if their new sense of place would have to be the new, suburban environments or if they would move on to what's left of other places similar to their old, rural surroundings.

We know there is no harm meant by the majority of people moving to the countryside. Their motives are mostly genuine and there are some who actually have a better grasp on respecting the land than do some of the long-term ruralites. It's just that eventually most of the rural landscape could disappear.

I've given great thought to what artists might best do to change trends and help find ways to balance the wants and needs of rural development with the need to preserve my familiar rural sense of place.

Maybe we need to be more descriptive about the beauty of our space and its people, so those "outsiders" wouldn't feel the need to make anything but mental visits without ever having to leave their urban and suburban homes.

Maybe we should suggest that people look at our work, but don't touch the subject.

Maybe we should tell about more of the bad that goes with all of the rural good. There are, after all, plenty of mosquitoes in the country. There are ticks around those woodlots. The grass people lie in to look at the sky makes you itch. The romance of our old country swimming holes comes complete with feet full of leeches. There are days when farms of all sizes stink up the air. Sometimes loud and incessant noises come from farm equipment or guns. A barefoot walk through the tall grass on an old farm can result in a tetanus shot after you step on an old, rusty nail in a board. The satisfaction of an honest day's work after baling hay often includes layers of blisters and prickly-bumps on your arms.

We want people to come. We want economic progress.

We don't want people to come. We don't want economic progress.

For now, I'll take the many questions out to a quiet space along our grand countryside and contemplate them. I'll listen to rustling leaves and the occasional song of a distant meadowlark.

Maybe I'll swat a bunch of mosquitoes and pick ticks from my body, too.

Only a Tractor

It was only a tractor.

Howard was watching as the cattle and machinery were about to be sold from his family farm, the farm that his father had taken over from his grandfather; the farm that he'd worked for many years and then had passed to one of his sons.

Everyone knew the sale was for the best. It was a necessary business decision, and his family was in full support of the son getting rid of what had become too much of a financial burden.

Howard also knew the sale would be the best way to handle the situation, making the cattle and machinery lower in value than the daily heartaches and headaches their continued use was causing him and his son.

In any other business, there would be a sale and the business owner would look for something else to do. There might be a small piece in the newspapers announcing the company is going out of business. But, after that, most business owners part with their companies' equipment without a qualm.

It's not the same on a farm, whether or not that's fair to the farmers. Many of them – especially those on multi-generational farms – spent every waking hour of their youth, every waking hour of their adult life and every

Roaming the Roads of Rural Life

waking hour of their elderly days on that farm. They always were there, at least in mind, if not in person.

Howard had come to know the most intimate secrets about every corner of the farm, its land and its animals. Every inch of the farm's land, from the most productive hillside land to the lowest part of its swamps, had been worked by Howard at one time or another. Cobwebs had been swept from every inch of the barn's ceiling, helping him learn every curve in the old barn's beams. He'd overseen the birth of every cow being milked and knew how to handle each of the cow's daily moods.

And then, there was the tractor.

He'd ridden that old tractor over every rut on the farm, and then some.

"I sort of got attached to that Farmall Super M," he said a couple of days before the auction. "I bought that new around 1950, and hate to see the damned thing go."

The Super M was one of the first new pieces of equipment he'd purchased after taking over the farm. He and a neighbor who shared equipment with the family had each purchased a new Super M, and it was quite a neighborhood event when an implement dealer unloaded them in the farm's yard.

The tractor had been the talk of the neighborhood back then, what with all of its power – "snoose" as Howard called it. The power pales in comparison with the average tractor used on today's farms, but back then it and the three-bottom plow it pulled were as much as any farmer imagined he'd need for quite some time. It was extra-special because of the "Super" designation that indicated a couple of more horsepower than found in the regular Farmall "M" series.

It was an all-purpose tractor for Howard, taking care of the majority of the farm's crop burdens. There were other tractors on the farm that were used in support of the Super M, but that tractor definitely was the quarterback of the farm's team of machinery.

Howard and his family's older children spent endless hours on that tractor, day and night, trying to beat each season's weather conditions. The younger children relished the thought of someday being allowed to perch themselves on the tractor's seat, already sensing the power that was associated with such a position.

It was overhauled a few times in its life, and painted at least twice. It identified the pride of Howard's operation like little else on the farm.

But the tractor was lined up along with the farm's other machinery. People ogled the Super M, sat on its seat and started it. The tractor to them might mean a few extra bucks made by reselling it as an antique. Or, maybe they would use it to haul a few loads of hay. They guessed that, if the bidding was right, they could find some use for what they believed must be little more than an old clunker.

Howard watched those people, knowing they meant well. But, he felt as though they were violating something by even looking at his tractor.

The bidding is over and the tractor is gone. It can be no more than a memory for the old man and his family.

The city-types at the local coffee shops generally look with wonder – and likely with some disdain – at such an attachment to a piece of steel and rubber. They wonder how someone could have become so attached to a piece of machinery that represents endless toil and labor.

For goodness sake, it's only a tractor, they said.

It's "only" a tractor, Howard agreed, knowing that sometimes only other farmers could understand his feelings for his beloved Super M.

He knew that, in its own way, that tractor represented all that he found good about his small piece of the rural world.

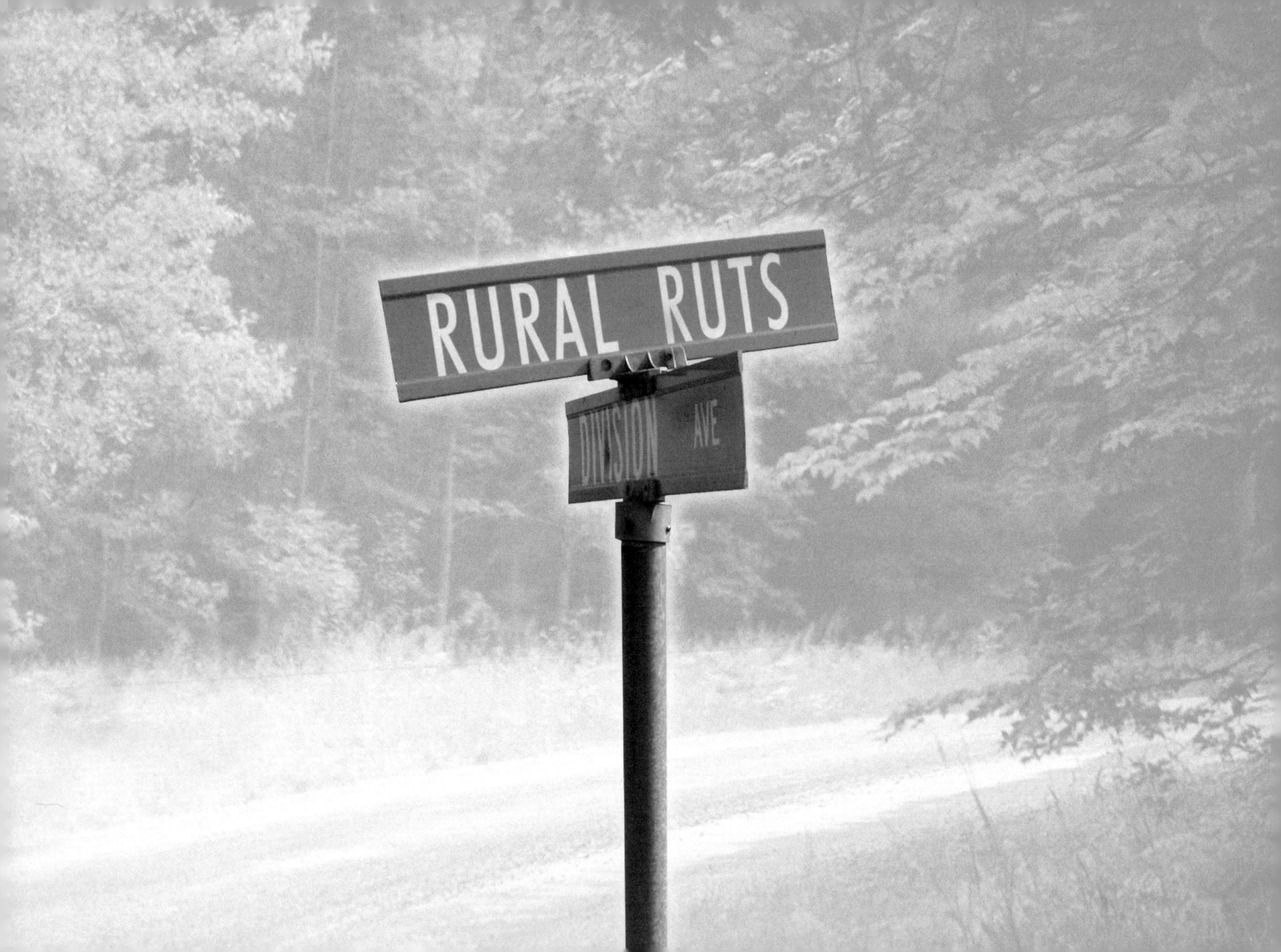
RURAL RUTS
DIVISION AVE

Rural Ruts

Staying in a Rut

The guy riding with me along one of Wisconsin's state highways sounded quite critical of the road's condition. He whined for many miles about the ruts in the road, and I'm pretty sure he could have received plenty of support for his views.

That highway was in pretty rough shape. The tires of the millions of vehicles that traveled on the road had left inch-deep grooves. Years of seasonal temperature swings from 100 degrees above zero to 45 degrees below caused cracks and potholes.

My friend was wrong about one thing, though. The road – in as bad of shape as it was – had no ruts.

I recalled a vice presidential candidate a few years ago who took offense to another candidate who apparently compared himself to John F. Kennedy.

"Sir, I knew Jack Kennedy, and you're not Jack Kennedy," the offended candidate said.

Likewise, in the car that day, I wanted to say, "Sir, I've known ruts, and these aren't ruts."

Grooves in highways are grooves in highways. Tracks left in the dirt are tracks left in the dirt. Ruts are ruts.

Rural people who have ever tried to harvest corn in the rainiest Wisconsin Septembers and Octobers know what ruts are. Ruts are what's left behind after a tractor, forage chopper and wagon have been buried up to their axles in the clammy-cold, clay-mixed loam – each having to be pulled to higher ground by one or two tractors linked with long logging chains.

The corn-harvesting ruts can be deep – very deep. Small children can disappear as they pass through such ruts; small animals have been known to enter them and never leave. Many a man, young or old, has crossed a cornfield in the nights following such a harvest and suddenly become face down on the cold soil, the mud pushing dampness up his shirt sleeves; knees hyperextended as his body continues forward and his feet lock into the rut's depth.

Falls into autumn corn-harvesting ruts are serious enough when they occur for any reason. But, they're especially treacherous in the dark of night for those who follow hounds in hunts for wild game of the night, such as raccoons.

It's good to quickly disk corn-harvesting ruts closed and into memory, because they can haunt the rural countryside through many frozen months and into the spring planting season.

Old-timers have spoken with reverence for the days of real ruts along their rural routes. In the days before paved rural roads, they were forced to pick and choose the days they could travel the roads because of the deep ruts. Narrow car tires and wagon wheels traveling the roads in the first third of the 20th century drove deep ruts into those unpaved byways.

Driving on a springtime rural road usually meant going the same way vehicles had previously traveled. The phrase "in a rut" undoubtedly evolved from the way those old-timers were forced to drive on the rutted roads – once they were in it, there wasn't much of a chance of getting out.

The most well known rural ruts created by animals are those made in lanes by dairy cows moving between pasture and barn. Those ruts start as simple tracks made by lines of cows following their leaders.

Days, months and then years of making those tracks – hooves each day driving an inch or two deeper into the soil – create ruts that are knee-deep to a grown man and thigh-deep to a boy.

There are dangers to humans who walk the cow-lane ruts. Some of the dangers are similar to those with fall cornfield ruts. But farm boys would say the benefits of walking in cow-lane ruts are much greater than the risks.

The benefits of walking those ruts can't always be understood by children who are directed to chase cows down the lanes every day. For many, the joys of the sights, sounds, smells and even feelings of those daily trips can't be realized until the lane-walking days are long past.

Old men's memories of navigating ruts in lanes are more valuable than gold; tastes of sweet grass they chewed in their cow-following days lingering for decades after the fact.

Rural ruts are dangerous; they're sometimes ugly. Rural routes bring challenges and they make for memories, good and bad.

Some are critical of those of us who don't mind staying in our rural ruts. I don't care.

Maybe, if more people learned the wonder of the deepest part of a rural rut, they'd stop sweating the small stuff. Maybe they'd even see a bit of joy in a few minor grooves in a highway.

Roaming the Roads of Rural Life

Acknowledgements

I've long maintained that all good writing comes straight from a writer's heart – that the writer's mind, bones and muscles only serve as tools to get the writing onto a page. But in compiling a book such as Rural Routes and Ruts, I've learned that it takes many people to make the project a reality.

My family, from my great-great grandparents to my grandchildren, have greatly influenced and driven what's on these pages. The best parts of my imagination can't fathom what my world would have been like or what this book's stories would be like without any of them.

The inspiration for some parts of Rural Routes and Ruts comes from writing I'd originally done for The Country Today or The Tribune-Record-Gleaner, two Wisconsin newspapers. Thanks to the leadership at both of the newspapers for allowing me to search archives to expand upon those original stories.

The Jim and Rhonda Dehnke family of Augusta, WI, deserves thanks for allowing me to use their farm – and themselves – for subjects of some of this book's photographs.

My good friend, Denise Beasley, spent countless hours editing my work and asked for nothing in return. Her objective view of my writing brought new insights into the book.

Thanks to the many others along the way who have given moral support to this effort.

Finally, thanks to my publishers, The Guest Cottage, for believing in this project and to TC Imaging for its design.

About the Author

Scott Schultz is a veteran journalist and newspaper editor raised on a central Wisconsin dairy farm, where he realized his interest in writing and journalism during high school.

He honed his writing skills while serving in the U.S. Marine Corps, and then returned to his Wisconsin roots to work in the newspaper business.

During his newspaper career, Schultz never forgot his rural roots and connection with the soil first tilled by his great-great grandfather. The resulting passion has led him to write hundreds of essays about that land and the people who share his love for life on the Rural Routes.

Schultz also has shared his love for writing by founding and developing a nonprofit project for writing and arts education.